# COOKING FROM THE
# HEART OF EUROPE

# COOKING FROM THE HEART OF EUROPE

*Food from Austria,*
*Hungary, Czechoslovakia,*
*and*
*South Germany*

## ROBIN HOWE

DAVID & CHARLES

NEWTON ABBOT  LONDON  VANCOUVER

Set in 11 on 13pt Bembo and printed in
Great Britain by Biddles Limited
Guildford for David & Charles
(Holdings) Limited South Devon House
Newton Abbot Devon

Published in Canada by Douglas David &
Charles Limited 3645 McKechnie Drive
West Vancouver BC

# CONTENTS

# INTRODUCTION

Austria, Czechoslovakia, Hungary and South Germany constitute what is generally considered as Central Europe, although there may be some people who disagree with this definition. These countries cover a large area through which runs a definite pattern of eating and cooking. Many of the recipes attributed to one country could equally be claimed by any of the others. But despite the similarities in this food pattern, each country expresses its own basic individuality.

Obviously I have not been able to include recipes for all their dishes, and I have therefore chosen those which please me most, which do not take up too much time, and are neither too complicated nor too difficult. It should not be hard to obtain the required ingredients.

Writing this book and eating my way through the many dishes has been something of a bitter-sweet pleasure—it revived so many memories. If I were to dedicate this book to anyone, it would be to those many friends I had—and still have—in Central Europe and to those who, for political reasons, must now live outside their own countries.

Porto Maurizio, Italy

# AUSTRIA

Until the end of World War I, Vienna was the capital of a sprawling empire and the Habsburg dynasty at one time held sway over much of Germany, the Netherlands, Poland, Hungary, Czechoslovakia, Yugoslavia, Rumania and northern Italy. The empire embraced not only a wide territory but also the many styles of cooking of the different peoples. The Austrians are quite willing to admit that many of their dishes come from their neighbours and erstwhile compatriots but, they add, these dishes, en route to Vienna, absorbed the special Austrian flavour: 'like a waltz in the frying pan, peppered with charm and sprinkled with high spirits'.

Austrians eat because they like to eat and not because they are hungry; most of them have given up the unequal struggle between eating and expanding waistlines. Not that they are over-fat, perhaps the German word *mollig* meaning comfortable or cosy applies to them best.

One eats both well and often in this food-conscious country. The day starts with rolls and butter, maybe an egg, or bread with honey, or ham, and coffee or chocolate. But as the day starts early, during the morning there is a stop for the second breakfast, which is quite a meal. If eaten in a restaurant, it might well be a small meat dish, maybe a goulash, or a plate of cold meats, or *Beuschal* which is minced offal, usually lights and lungs served with a dumpling, or *Beinfleisch*, boiled beef with fresh horseradish, or frankfurter sausages with sauerkraut or a mustard sauce. If the second breakfast is eaten in the office, then out come important looking briefcases which look as though they contain high priority documents but actually reveal the far more important fresh rolls stuffed with meat or sausages.

Around midday, off go the Austrians for lunch, a meal of meat, vegetables and a sweet dish. An hour or so after lunch, hunger again creeps in and it is time for *Jause*. It is lightly called a 'mid-afternoon snack' but just wander into any of Austria's pastry shops and you will see what this little snack means: a thoroughly good tuck-in to cakes filled with cream. *Jause* stretches from 3 to 5pm but soon after 6 o'clock the Austrians are ready to tackle dinner, much the same as the luncheon menu. And finally, just before retiring to bed, another light snack is taken for, after all, one could wake up with night starvation. I have seen people attacking a large plate of boiled meats or frankfurters with sauerkraut as early as 7am. And by 8am the chickens and roasts are already grilled ready for taking away.

Although Vienna is not Austria, one tends to talk of the capital when considering Austrian food. Naturally it is a city where one can find every type of food, national and international. Austria and Vienna does not only mean *Wiener Schnitzel*—far from it. Although this is a favourite meat dish, not many realise that its origin was Italian or that Field Marshal Radetsky, reporting on the progress of the Italian campaign, also wrote enthusiastically of the Milanese veal escalopes. On the Emperor's orders he personally demonstrated the dish to the royal chefs and so well was the lesson learnt that *costoletta alla Milanese* found itself renamed *Wiener Schnitzel* and naturalised. Pork *Schnitzels* are also popular, and there are *Schnitzels* with mussels, anchovies, and nowadays even with a curry sauce.

Another important, indeed aristocratic, dish is the *Tafelspitz* (see page 73) or boiled beef. This was a favourite of Emperor Franz Josef and, as he reigned for almost seventy years, the *Tafelsptiz* became the most important dish in all noble households. The meat used is the finest cut of prime beef which is cooked gently for several hours until tender and is served with a variety of sauces and vegetables according to season. It is the sauces which really make this rather ordinary dish a gourmet's choice.

In Austria, pork is cooked almost with reverence; after this comes beef which more often than not is boiled. Veal is braised, roasted and stuffed, used for *Schnitzels* and goulash; lamb is almost never eaten. Offal plays an important role in the Austrian kitchen and poultry means chicken. These birds are fried, grilled, boiled, roasted, stuffed—there seems to be no limit to what an Austrian can do with a chicken. Duck, turkey, goose also have their adherents, and goose is the traditional Christmas bird.

Game meat, though not as popular as pork or beef, is cooked in every possible manner and not a bit of it is wasted. Lesser cuts of venison, for example, are made into stews or goulashes. Dumplings, rice and pasta are the usual accompaniments.

Austrians are no exception to the Central European preference for freshwater fish but generally speaking the Viennese are suspicious of fish, odd for a city with so many street names beginning witlr *Fischer*.

Much of Austria's culinary fame is based on doughs and these include the pastries for which Austrians have been famous since the seventeenth century. Other dishes are those produced from flour and are mostly sweet puddings. Austria has made the *Strüdel* so much part of their cuisine that most people consider it an Austrian speciality, much to the annoyance of the Hungarians who have been making *Rètes* or *Strüdel* for centuries. *Sachertorte* and *Linzertorte*, however, are truly Austrian and hold a special reputation. Vienna certainly seems to have more shops filled with exquisite pastries and cakes than any other city in the world.

Apart from the great restaurants and hotels, there are a large number of different kinds of eating establishments all over Austria. Quite often the Austrian name for a particular type of eating house is not possible to translate, like the *Beisel*. This is the lowest category of eating house and rarely discovered by foreigners, but it is where the Viennese are at home. Then there is the *Gasthaus* or inn where usually the innkeeper's wife does the cooking. Here, too, the fare is modest but good and in the country not only does the wife cook the food but she often grows or rears it as well. There are the *Burgerlischen*—middle-class or family—restaurants, where the fare is more varied, usually more traditional than that found in the international restaurants but of a high quality.

Coffee is the non-alcoholic drink of the Austrians and the history of the Viennese coffee houses goes back to the Turk's unsuccessful siege of the city in 1683. On retreating, they left behind some strange, black-looking beans. No one knew what to do with them except a merchant named Kolschitzy. He asked to be given the beans and made black coffee from them in the Turkish style—and sold it to the Viennese. Today the coffee houses are still something of an institution in Vienna, although perhaps not as popular as they were in more leisurely times.

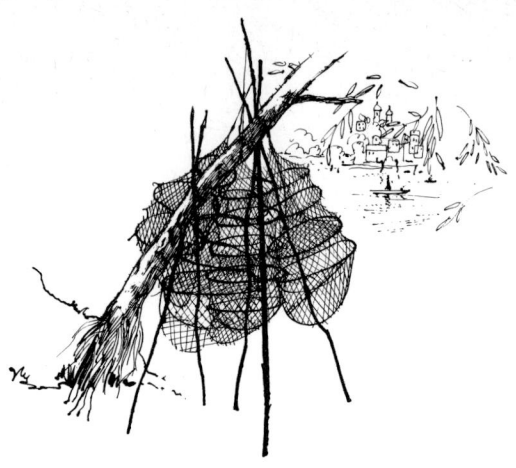

# CZECHOSLOVAKIA

Goethe described Bohemia as 'a continent within a continent' because the country was shut off from its neighbours by mountains on three sides; only the way to the east lay open. The country we call Czechoslovakia was created after World War I and then comprised Bohemia, Moravia, Slovakia, Austrian Silesia and Ruthenia. The recently formed Czechoslovakia Republic no longer includes Ruthenia.

According to Czech chronicles, the ancestral chief of their country was a man called Čech, who led his people from far distant lands until they reached the mountain called Řip in Bohemia. Here he found a rich and fertile land abounding in game and fish, so he decided to settle there. The modern Czech national anthem describes their country as 'looking like an earthly paradise'.

Foreign writers have added to this picture. The word Bohemia, wrote an American some years ago, 'stands for something more than music, art and gay living. The Bohemian kitchen with its Slovak additions has long been the centre and heart geographically and gastronomically of European culinary art.' Well, not everyone may accept this praise but I think the Czechs certainly believed it.

However, to be fair, from a country comprising so many nationalities it can hardly be expected that it should possess a typical Czech 'kitchen'. The peoples of this region each had their own style of cooking and remained faithful to their regional specialities. Also centuries old trade routes traversed the country and left their mark on the local cooking. Many foreign dishes have crept in and now form part of the national cuisine. Indeed, many Czechs would find it difficult to give the origin of many of their favourite foods.

Czechoslovakia was reputed for its cakes and cookies and the average Czech cookbook contains more recipes for sweet dishes than it does for meat or savoury ones. There are sponge cakes filled with thick whipped cream; rich tarts with fillings of fruits or preserves; there are all kinds of breads, many sweet and skilfully plaited and served only at certain festivals; doughnuts and fried pastries; poppy seed cakes, delicious honey cakes and gingerbreads. Internationally known are *oplatky* (oblaten) or wafers which started life as thin small church wafers, and were developed in Carlsbad into plate-sized, sugared wafers, the recipe for which was long kept a secret. Almost as well known are *Lomnický suchar* (Lomnitz Zwieback).

At Christmas, the Czech housewife turned her attention to the baking of traditional cookies, usually making more than twenty varieties. Easter meant gingerbread cake-loaf and beautifully hand-painted eggs, the most beautiful coming from Slovakia. St Nicholas' Day meant a plate of dried fruit and cookies, oranges and nuts for those children who had been good all the year round. For those who had been bad, the plate held coal and wood.

After cakes in the Czech culinary hierarchy come dumplings, as much part of the Czech cuisine as the people themselves. And what variety there is, ranging from the filling but good bread or potato dumplings to those as light as a soufflé. They come in every conceivable shape and size, round and small, large and fluffy, sweet and savoury, rich and plain, and so on *ad infinitum*. They are served as a main course, with or without an accompaniment, or in soup or as a sweet dish. Some are very large, others the size of a pea, but generally they are the size of a tennis ball. Indeed, the variety of the dumpling is limited only by the imagination of the cook and some dumpling recipes have been in Czech families for generations, not to be shared for love or money. A good dumpling recipe used to be part of a young girl's dowry.

Sausages constitute a cult in Czechoslovakia and many were (maybe still are) the subject of fierce arguments on the relative merits of the sausage makers. One famous Prague institution was the *uzenářství*, a meat shop selling sausages, salami, smoked hams and meats, and providing customers with small tables or a good-sized counter at which they could sit with a great mug of Pilsner beef (*Plzeňské pivo*) and a plate of hot or cold sausage eaten with a mustard or horseradish sauce. This was the second breakfast, served not only in the more plebeian eating houses but also in the first-class restaurants and hotels. The *uzenářství* were very much part of the Prague way of living. Every morning around 10 o'clock they would be packed with customers and there would be others collecting a large snack to take back to colleagues confined to their desks. In the streets of old Prague there were the *výčep* bars where the clientèle stood at a counter with beer and fresh rolls generally filled with cheese or meat. These were the meeting places of the local tradesmen and artisans.

Pork is the favourite meat of the Czechs and their national dish is still roast pork served with sauerkraut and noodles or dumplings. Their most important pork product is the Prague ham, *Pražska šunka*, shipped all over the world and considered by many connoisseurs the finest of all hams. It is salted and cured in brine for several months, after which it is lightly smoked over beech wood and then kept in a cool cellar until marketed. Lamb, kid and beef also are popular meats.

Geese are reared in enormous numbers and, in the past, the goose girls and boys were a familiar sight as they paraded with their unwieldy herds. Geese are force fattened, as in France, to produce over-large livers and plenty of flesh. Roast goose, stuffed goose necks, larded goose liver and goose pâté were regular items on the Czech festive tables. Another favourite was goose giblets cooked in paprika, surely of Hungarian origin.

Like other countries in Central Europe, Czechoslovakia relies on fresh-water fish which the rivers and lakes provide in good quantities. First favourite is carp, and Christmas Eve without its dish of carp served in a rich black sauce is a sorry day.

But all Czech cooking is not sausages, dumplings and cakes. There are thick nourishing soups and plenty of vegetables. Probably the potato is the favourite Czech vegetable but the cabbage comes a close second and not far behind are mushrooms. It is claimed there are hundreds of different mushroom varieties which grow abundantly in woods and forests. Many, such as the edible boletus, are dried and preserved for leaner times. They are made into salads and served as light supper dishes with eggs, or in a cream sauce.

# HUNGARY

To judge by Hungarian cookery books, the whole of Hungarian history is filled with culinary lore and much of it is very entertaining. Many of the Hungarian cookbook writers delve into the very beginnings of the nation, back to the nomad heathens who stormed through Europe striking fear wherever they rested. In a church in Modena in Italy, they prayed: '*De sagittis Hungarorum, libera nos, Domine*, Oh Lord, save us from the arrows of the Hungarians'. But when the Hungarian hordes overran an ancient monastery in St Gallen, in Switzerland, and all but one monk named Heribald fled, he recorded that they were good people and pleasant company—with healthy appetites.

The nomads settled in Central Europe and settled wisely, for the great Hungarian plains were highly productive, even during the periods of long and hard wars, and became the granary of Europe.

During the years of Austro-Hungarian monarchy, there was a great mixing of the national cuisines but generally the Hungarians kept to their own style of living and most definitely to the pattern of their cooking. Austria turned towards the west and remained classic, correct and conservative. Hungary turned towards the east whence much of her cooking came and retained a strong Magyar influence. While Austria danced to Strauss waltzes, Hungary listened to the haunting tones of her gipsies.

By the nineteenth century, Hungarian cooking had reached its zenith and Hungarian cooks and chefs travelled widely in Europe, especially in France, and brought back new ideas which somewhat refined the good, but nevertheless countryfied, Hungarian cooking. These cooks claimed they took from the French but did not copy their recipes, but whether they did or not, the standard of cooking both in restaurants and homes did develop and it was a proud boast that it was easier to find a white raven in Hungary than a Hungarian housewife who could not cook. However, one writer explained that cooking was not an art confined only to the women, for the preparation of a *gulyàs* was a man's work.

The culinary evolution of Hungary was also assisted by royal marriages. Matthias Corvinus in the fifteenth century married an Italian princess, Beatrice de Este, who reputedly brought Italian recipes with her and introduced cheese, onions, garlic and dill into Hungary. At the time of Maria Theresa and her son, Joseph II, the royal table and those of the aristocracy were almost entirely French.

Another interesting influence on Hungarian cooking is the Turkish. The Turks, who conquered the country in the sixteenth and seventeenth centuries, brought with them, from Spain, paprika or sweet pepper. This became a Hungarian vegetable and it was the Hungarians who developed the art of drying it and using it in the form of a powdered condiment which the Turks do not. However, the use of paprika pepper did not take on quickly. Most Hungarians would generally be surprised to know that its use in cooking is not more than a century old.

However, it was in Transylvania where the great Magyar families remained sublimely indifferent to outside influences in their kitchens that the cooking was considered of the finest, maintaining tradition and the true, ancient dishes of Hungary.

There is one subject on which all Hungarians agree whatever their age or their political opinions, and that is the quality of their food and the superiority of their dishes. Cakes and pastries? 'There is no need to recommend them; they are unsurpassed,' wrote one culinary expert. And, 'it goes without saying that our bread and rolls are of the finest quality', a quality due to the good fortune of the Hungarians in having the right land and climate to grow a gluten-rich wheat yielding a flour of high flavour and richness. It is with this flour that the *rètes* (*Strüdel*) pastry is made; also the delicious but tricky-to-make *Dobos Torta*, a cake named after a famous Hungarian pastry chef. With this same flour noodles, breads, pastries and dumplings are made.

What constitutes the traditional *gulyàs*? Kàroly Gundel, descendant of a famous Hungarian restaurateur and chef, explains it for us. There are four kinds of dishes in which paprika pepper is an important ingredient, all rather similar and all apt to be classed either by laziness or ignorance as *gulyàs*. Here they are, the four most important meat dishes of the country.

*Gulyàs.* A dish of meat cut into stew-sized pieces and cooked with plenty of liquid, onions, paprika pepper, potatoes and home-made noodles or small dumplings. A *gulyàs* is made with beef or chicken, seldom with mutton or pork. But there is one exception to this rule, the *Szekelygulyàs* which is made either with mixed meats, or only with pork. It is more a ragoût than a soup.

*Pörkölt.* In this, finely chopped onions play an important part and the gravy is thick, like a sauce, otherwise it resembles a *gulyàs*.

*Tokàny.* In this the meat is cut into smaller cubes and less onion and paprika is used. Mushrooms, green peas and carrots can be added, also fresh or sour cream.

*Paprikàs.* This name is applied to almost any dish well flavoured with paprika pepper and to which sour or fresh cream is added. Usually it is reserved for white meats, fowl, veal and lamb, also for fish and potatoes. Red meats, game, geese, duck and pork are not used for *paprikàs*.

If the Hungarians are convinced of the superiority of their cooking, it is nothing to the pride they have for their freshwater fish, in particular the *fogas* from Lake Balaton. It is the perch-pike or, more exactly, *lucioperca sandra* and indeed a splendid fish.

Another ingredient without which the Hungarian cannot cook is sour cream, although for finer cooking fresh cream is preferred. It was explained to me that to cook Hungarian food without sour cream is like life without love.

# SOUTH GERMANY

Up till World War II, Germany had been unified for only seventy-three years, and the once separate countries have maintained their national characteristics, their own food customs and their cooking.

South Germany, like every other part of the world, is changing and it would be foolish to suppose that travelling within the region one will be served only sauerkraut and dumplings and what may seem local and oddly named dishes. A great deal of international cooking is done, particularly in the more expensive town restaurants and another interesting trend is the call for dishes of the Orient. Though I suspect that few Orientals would recognise many of the dishes attributed to their countries, it is understandable that when Germans eat out they want to try something mother does not make.

Yet another aspect to remember when considering German eating today is that figure control has entered into the reckoning. To a great extent the Germans always were interested in losing weight for, while they seemed to eat astonishingly well, they would go off regularly to a *Kurhaus* to get rid of the surplus fat—then blithely start eating all over again.

Generally speaking, eating in Germany is not a hurried performance, except during the short luncheon hour in towns when most people do eat fairly quickly. But by habit the German likes to eat and drink with some deliberation, and in Bavaria with positive exuberation.

The day in South Germany starts with the first breakfast to be followed by the second one, a much more important meal. In Baden this appears as early as 9 o'clock and in local dialect is called *z'nüni*, or nines. It consists of rye bread with some smoked raw bacon served with cherry brandy, a little hard for my stomach to accept so early. However, this combination can be tried as a lunch starter, followed by poached trout or an egg salad.

Most main meals start with a soup. Winter brings thick, warming soups; summer, thin soups with varying garnishes. There are wine, beer and fruit soups, the latter, called *Kaltschale*, are usually served cold, often with a garnish of egg white or snow dumplings. They can be made with all kinds of fruit, with apples and cherries as first favourites.

Fish means freshwater fish cooked simply but with a strong preference for fish cooked blue. In Bavaria one finds the *Isarhuchen*, a member of the salmon family which is popular, so also is the *Waller*, a fish only caught in the tributaries of the Danube.

Pork undoubtedly is the most popular meat, but closely followed by boiled beef. Southern Germans, in particular *Müncheners*, love game. As it is a lean meat, a game glutton has less fear for his figure. In some of the large hotels pheasants are preserved by deep freezing so this favourite game bird can be served as late as March.

When in Germany, I am never in doubt of the justness of their claim to over 1,000 varieties of sausage. Germans too are fond of plates of cold meat and in many homes where the main hot meal of the day is the midday one, the evening meal often consists of cold meat or sausages thinly sliced and served with different sauces. But not all sausages are eaten sliced or cold: a great many are fried and others, in particular white sausages, are boiled and served with sauerkraut. Munich is particularly proud of its white sausage. Baden produces its Swabian *Schlachtplatte*, a powerful dish of sauerkraut, dumplings, liver, blood and white sausages and pease pudding.

Apart from cabbage and potatoes, the next most popular vegetable is probably the mushroom of which there are so many varieties, including the tiny champignons, *Steilpilz*, and the funny little *Pfefferling*. And asparagus, how the Germans love this fine vegetable. There is an asparagus-and-opera-festival combined in Schwetzingen. A good South German dish is asparagus with boiled tongue and ham. German salads by no means are restricted to lettuce, tomatoes and cucumbers.

German cheeses are not inspiring—most of them are a pale copy of a cheese from a neighbouring country. But bread is quite another matter and a never-ending joy for bread connoisseurs.

Like most of the peoples in Central Europe, the Germans like cakes and southern Germany is a paradise for the sweet-toothed with its rich layered cakes stuffed with cream, cheese cakes, seldom without cream these days, fruit tarts and flans, and a riot of small cakes or cookies plus enormous marzipan confections.

Munich is the most important city in the region and, as far as its residents are concerned, the centre of German gastronomy. A first impression of the centre of Munich is that it is *en fête*. The roads teem with Bavarians running hither and thither all going about, as one discovers later, the important business of coping with the demands of the inner man. For in between the main meals of the day it is recognised that a man must eat so, on the hour, he takes a little meal known as a *Schmankerl*, described as 'enough to eat but not to completely satisfy' the appetite.

The day begins with coffee, rolls and butter, honey or preserves and often cheese. This keeps the *Münchener* going until 10 o'clock, although some may have already had a 9am *Schmankerl*, when they all attack a meal called *Brotzeit*. Although this can be taken at any time of the morning, the 10 o'clock one is the most important for it is then that *Leberkäse* (liver-cheese) is eaten. And this oddly named dish is a meat loaf made from mixed meats, onions and spices and contains neither cheese nor liver. Freshly baked every morning, it comes out of the pan with a rich thick crust and is cut into large slices. It is eaten with bread and naturally accompanied with a mug of beer.

This sustains that inner man until about 11 o'clock when *Weisswurste* or white sausages are served and must be consumed before the *Rathaus* clock chimes 12 noon.

There is a snobbery about how you eat *Weisswurste*, as indeed with most of the boiled sausages. The best advice one can give to foreigners is to look around and watch the local fellows at work. As far as the *Münchener* is concerned, he who cuts his sausage lengthwise or eats it with French mustard is indeed a barbarian who comes from the wrong side of the River Isar. The correct mustard sauce is made from two kinds of mustard.

The afternoon is not without its time for food, for there is the *Vesper* or

*Jause*, afternoon tea with plenty of creamy cakes, and also a time for having a coffee or a beer. After dinner and just before turning into bed, *Müncheners* feel the need for another beer and, to give them enough strength to actually get them to bed, they take a little snack, or *Betthupfer*, (bed hopper). How they manage through the night is not officially stated but I suppose they can, like some Austrians, creep downstairs and raid the larder.

# GENERAL INFORMATION

The items below have been placed in alphabetical order for easy reference.

**Bacon**   Whenever bacon is used in recipes it refers to the thickly sliced, very fat, Continental-type available in most good stores. American readers should note that it is *not* the heavily salted and smoked fat bacon to be found in most supermarkets.

**Bread**   The Germans claim to bake several hundred different varieties of bread, and the Austrians are not far behind. The splendid displays plus the aroma of freshly baked bread coming from the bakers' shops demoralises those attempting a diet. Much of the bread of this region is dark, usually made with rye flour or a mixture of wheat and rye flours. Much of it is flavoured with caraway seeds or sprinkled with poppy seeds. Some white bread also is sprinkled with poppy seeds. White bread is much in demand, in the shape of breakfast rolls and for toasting as well as for making sandwiches.

The Viennese are justly noted for the quality of their breakfast rolls. The Germans produce considerable quantities of packaged, sliced breads made with rye flour (of the *Pumpernickel* type) which are extremely good and have a long lasting quality. They are especially good with curd cheese. The Austrians make excellent croissants and some people consider them better than their French rivals. However, neither country can claim the origin of the croissant for this belongs to Hungary.

In many recipes in this book a bread roll is called for. This is what the Austrians call a *Semmel* and is the same size as the average roll sold in Britain and the United States, about 4oz of bread. When travelling in Austria and southern Germany on a Sunday, do not be surprised when given cake or a sweet bread for breakfast instead of the usual fresh roll. Bakers do not bake on Saturday night.

**Buttered breadcrumbs**   A garnish for pies, cauliflower etc made by browning soft, fresh crumbs in hot butter. Will keep for a short while if not used immediately.

**Caraway seeds**  A popular flavouring in Central Europe, especially in South Germany and Austria where they seem to be used in almost every dish, but very much in the making of breads. Used particularly with pork, sauerkraut, cabbage and in *gulyàs*.

**Celeriac**  A large, rather ugly root vegetable which is nevertheless a true celery and grown for its root rather than the stalk; the latter can be cooked and served like sea-kale. Before using, it must be scrubbed, then thinly and carefully peeled.

**Curd** or **Cottage cheese**  The type of curd or white cheese called for in these recipes must be firm and dry, neither cream nor half cream. Most delicatessen stores sell this type of curd cheese, especially those run by Central Europeans and Poles. Also the Italian *ricotta* can be used.

**Dumplings**  These are served throughout Central Europe and included among dumplings are often some of the noodle shapes, varying from tiny, marble-sized soup garnishes to large fat 'sausages' cooked in a white cloth. Generally they are round, about the size of a tennis ball and made with flour, potatoes, semolina, or a mixture of them all. But there also are liver, egg and curd cheese dumplings. They come sweet or savoury, sometimes served as a sweet course or as a main course, following the soup.

**Fat for cooking**  Most Central Europeans prefer to cook with pork or goose fat although the Austrians prefer butter. It is possible to buy thick chunks of white pork fat in many delicatessen shops usually called by its German name *Speck*. This makes an admirable cooking fat when rendered down. Goose fat is less easily found but I have used chicken fat, usually obtainable in Jewish food shops which often also sell goose fat.

**Fish**  Central Europe is a land-locked region and sea fish obviously is not much in demand. The many lakes, rivers, mountain streams and ponds are rich in freshwater fish yielding carp, trout, a species of salmon, pike, perch, etc. There is a great demand, however, for the heavily salted and dried fish generally from Norway, and for herrings and similar fish kept in a vinegar brine, such as Bismarck herrings, rollmops and the like.

**Flour**  For making pastries and breads, Central Europeans prefer to use a strong flour, usually available in good grocery shops as well as the health food stores. Unless specified, self-raising flour is not used in the recipes in this book.

**Garlic**  Peeling garlic sometimes can be tricky. Try holding the point of the concave side downwards against a plate and gently push down with the thumb. Usually the flesh will snap loose from its paper-like casing. To crush garlic cloves, put them one at a time under the flat blade of a strong kitchen knife and press hard. This is better than using a garlic presser which so often seems to retain most of the garlic and send out the rest in a liquid form—which is not what is required.

**Horseradish**   Horseradish is a longish root and exceedingly pungent. It should be grated immediately before using or it will lose its pungency. If fresh horseradish cannot be found, the next best thing is commercially dried horseradish. Grating horseradish probably causes more tears than dealing with onions.

**Meat**   One of the problems facing the writer of foreign recipes is attempting to give the precise cuts of meat required for a particular dish. This is because cuts of meat differ in almost every country in the world. Much of the meat sold in Central Europe is de-boned. However, in the recipes in this book I have made suggestions as to the best cuts of meat to use. When in doubt consult your butcher.

**Mushrooms**   Many are the varieties of edible mushrooms and fungus found in the forests of Central Europe. Not all are found outside their usual habitat. However, in those recipes calling for mushrooms, almost any type of mushroom can be used. The flavour will be different but the dish will still be good.

**Onions**   Onions vary considerably in flavour, some being much more pungent than others. Central Europeans prefer red onions in many of their stews; in other dishes milder, sweeter onions are called for. But not all greengrocers have a choice. For frying and baking, a not too strongly flavoured onion is the best. When a recipe calls for the onion to be cooked until soft but not brown, this piece of advice should not be ignored. If onions are allowed to brown, they will be stronger in flavour thus giving a dominant flavour to a dish when this is not required. When in season, spring or green onions should be used in salads and in those cooked dishes requiring only the mildest onion flavour.

**Paprika pepper**   This is a bright red powder made from a particular species of pepper which is free from the pungency of chilli. In some cases, in order to reduce pungency still further, the seeds and cores are removed so that the powder is made only from the dried flesh. It is bland and almost sweet in flavour. When paprika pepper is fresh its colour is brilliant; if it is brown it is stale. There are various grades of pungency not

always available except in speciality food shops. It should be used in fairly
liberal quantities and is considered healthy on account of its high Vitamin
C content. The main types of paprika are:

1 Sweet (*Èdes paprika*), mild, almost sweet and used for *gulyàs*, *pörkölt*,
etc.

2 Half Sweet (*Fèl-èdes paprika*), a somewhat sharp paprika used by those
with a taste for the more piquant flavours.

3 Rose Paprika (*Rozsa paprika*), definitely sharp in flavour and used
only when a strong flavour is called for.

4 Hot Paprika (*Erös paprika*), used like pepper, in small quantities. It is
mainly found as a table condiment when dishes have been flavoured
with any of the other paprika peppers. The flavour of paprika is
brought out best in hot, but not boiling, fat—preferably pork fat. If
the fat is too hot, the paprika burns, browns and becomes bitter and
—in the case of sweet paprika—loses its aroma.

**Parsley root** or **Hamburg parsley**   A true parsley but grown for its
root which looks like a small parsnip. Its flavour is something between
parsley and celery and when unavailable, a parsnip is the next best thing.

**Poppy seeds**   There are many kinds of poppy seeds which come from
the opium poppy and, as they contain no alkaloids, they are an important
food. The seeds most usually found in Central Europe are blue-grey and
they are mainly used in confectionery and also with noodles and dumplings. Before using, they must be pounded in a mortar or ground in a
grinder.

**Sauerkraut**   Shredded, crisp white cabbage fermented in salt and
flavoured with caraway and juniper berries. Considered a German
invention, it in fact came from China via the Tartars to the Austrians,
who gave it its name. When possible, purchase fresh from the barrel;
otherwise use canned sauerkraut.

**Sausages**   The many varieties of sausages throughout the region are
made with pure meat, usually with pork but some with a mixture of meats.
The display of sausages in street markets, supermarkets and delicatessen
stores has been described as a sausage-eater's dreamland. Great mounds
from the palest pink to red of the deepest dye; sausages for frying, boiling,
grilling, for slicing and eating with a plate of cold meats, or in sandwiches,
or indeed just by themselves.

Many are spiced, some are flavoured with herbs, others are completely bland. Stores in Britain and the United States, as well as in other parts of the world, today sell a fascinating assortment of continental sausages.

**Sour cream**　Lavish use is made of sour cream in much Central European cooking, particularly in Hungary and Czechoslovakia. Sour cream can be bought in most delicatessen shops, good grocery stores and supermarkets. Fresh cream left in the refrigerator will also nicely sour if left for about a week. However, fresh cream can be used in its place if preferred.

**Sweet peppers** or **Capsicum**　Usually these are red, green or yellow, occasionally a mixture of all colours. They are of varying sizes, even shapes. Most of them have a large core with hundreds of very pepper-hot seeds but there are sweet peppers entirely devoid of seeds and cores and these usually are very sweet. Although most sweet peppers are, as their name implies, sweet and not pepper-hot, it does happen from time to time that an innocent looking pepper is extremely pungent. It is not possible to tell from the outside. Always remember that it is the seeds which contain the fire and be sure to discard them all. After dealing with sweet peppers, do remember not to lick your fingers, for the seeds will have passed on their fire.

**Vanilla sugar**　Something which every Central European cook has on hand. Replacing vanilla essence or flavourings it gives the dish in which it is used sufficient vanilla taste, lingering but not too strong. Make by adding broken up pods to large jar of sugar, cover tightly and shake well. Do not use for at least one month.

# A NOTE

When writing a cookery book intended for both British and American readers one comes across some slight differences of language. In the following recipes I have tried to use words common to both, such as the American 'can' instead of the British 'tin', as both sides of the Atlantic recognise the can. Then we have blender or liquidiser. Here I have preferred the British word liquidiser, as it seems to me more explanatory and American readers would more easily recognise liquidiser than the British would blender. In other cases I have given both words, the American equivalent in brackets.

In giving the metric measurement with the Imperial, I have given approximate measurements rather than absolute conversions as this is far easier for the average cook and the differences are slight enough to make no difference to the finished dish.

As far as cake or pastry measuring is concerned, I have tried to keep the proportions accurate. Also I see no reason to go into small quantities such as millilitres. No one does in the metric world and few of our kitchen scales weigh such tiny quantities accurately. Spoon measurements are used throughout Europe as indeed are cups and glasses. All spoon measurements throughout the recipes are level unless otherwise specified.

To enable readers on both sides of the Atlantic to use these recipes, and also to ensure that they are equally applicable when metrication is introduced, the ingredients throughout are given in the order: Imperial, followed by metric and US measures in parentheses. Where measurements are the same in the list of ingredients, eg British and continental spoon measurements, and British and US weight measurements, they are not always repeated.

| Abbreviations | teaspoon | tsp | gram | g |
| used: | tablespoon | tb | kilogram | kg |
| | ounce | oz | decilitre | dl |
| | pound | lb | litre | l |
| | pint | pt | centimetre | cm |
| | inch | in | | |

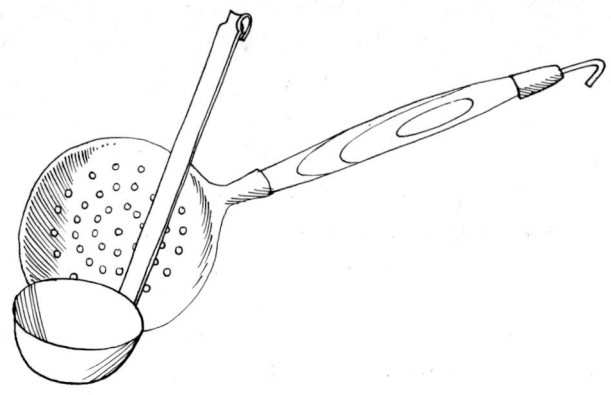

# SOUPS

### CLEAR BROTH WITH EGG (*Bouillon mit Ei*)   Austria

No exact quantities are needed for this simple soup. Crack open shell and slide one whole egg or egg yolk into a soup bowl or plate and then pour boiling hot clear broth over it. The heat from the broth sets the outer layer of the egg and, as you eat the soup, you stir the egg into it.

For the broth or stock used in this and the following recipes, see the recipe for Boiled Beef (*Tafelspitz*) on page 73. Beef bones may be used instead of meat to make stock. Ask the butcher to chop these for you.

### THICK BROWN SOUP (*Einbrennsuppe*)   Austria

4–6 servings:
3oz (90g,6tb) fat
3oz (90g,¾cup) flour
3pt (1¾l,4pt) stock
½pt (1¼l,1¼cups) red wine
2 egg yolks
3tb (4tb) cream or top of the milk
2tb parsley, 1tsp chives, finely chopped
salt, pepper to taste

Heat the fat, add the flour and stir the mixture to a roux. Continue cooking over a low heat for at least 30 minutes stirring frequently until the roux gives off a rich nutty aroma. Gradually add the stock, stirring all the time until the soup is thick. Bring gently to the boil, add wine, stir well, lower the heat and cook for 45 minutes.

About 5 minutes before soup is ready, beat the egg yolks into the cream, add the parsley, chives, salt and pepper. Gradually add 1 cupful of the hot soup, stirring all the time to prevent curdling. Return mixture to pan and stir it well into the soup. Continue cooking, stirring all the time until the soup has been reheated but do not allow it to boil.

This soup is one of many considered excellent for curing a hangover.

### BEEF AND CABBAGE SOUP (*Hovězi polévka s kapustou*)
### Czechoslovakia

6 servings:
1lb (½kg,1lb) stewing beef or steak
1 large firm white cabbage
4pt (2¼l,5pt) water
salt, pepper to taste
2oz (60g,¼cup) rice

Bring the water to the boil. Add the beef, salt and pepper, lower the heat and cook for 2½ to 3 hours. If the water is too much reduced, extra *boiling* water may be added but the liquid must never go off its simmering boil. Meanwhile, wash the cabbage, discard bruised leaves and hard stalks and shred finely.

When the meat is tender, take it from the pan and shred it into small pieces. Return it, with the cabbage and rice, to the pan. Bring to the boil and cook until rice is soft, 10 to 15 minutes.

This type of soup is popular throughout Central Europe and is served as a main dish with plenty of dark country bread. Some cheese, fruit or a salad would be sufficient to follow.

## GOULASH SOUP (*Gulyàs leves*)  Hungary

4–6 servings:
1lb (½kg,1lb) brisket
½lb (¼kg,½lb) onions, peeled and finely chopped
3tsp (4tsp) paprika pepper
salt to taste
1lb (½kg,1lb) potatoes
1 large tomato

Wipe the meat and cut it into cubes. Put meat, onions, paprika and salt into a pan. Cover with water, bring gently to the boil, lower the heat and continue cooking until the meat is almost tender. Meanwhile, peel the potatoes and cut into cubes. When the meat is cooked, add the potatoes and enough extra water to make enough soup for 4 to 6 servings. Continue cooking slowly until the potatoes are soft. Peel, and chop the tomato and add it to the soup just before serving.

This soup, the classical goulash, is usually served with tiny dumplings (*galuska* see page 130) which are added 2 minutes before serving.

## BEAN SOUP (*Bableves*)  Hungary

Here are two recipes for this very important Hungarian soup, often served as a main dish and also in the early hours of the morning after an all-night session. The first recipe is for those with a solid fuel burning stove; the second uses canned brown beans.

### Method 1

6 servings:
1lb (½kg,1lb) brown or red beans
3oz (90g,6tb) lard, chicken or goose fat
1–2 large onions, peeled and coarsely chopped
2oz (60g,½cup) flour
1–2 garlic cloves, chopped

2tsp paprika pepper
salt to taste
1lb ($\frac{1}{2}$kg,1lb) smoked pork or ham, chopped
6pt (3$\frac{1}{4}$l,7$\frac{1}{2}$pt) water

Soak the beans for 12 hours. Next day, drain and put with the remaining
ingredients into a large pan; cover and simmer for as long as possible
either on top of the stove or in a slow oven overnight. The soup should
be simmered for at least 12 hours and 24 is not too long.

## Method 2

Use a large can of red or brown beans preserved in water, not in a sauce.
Heat the fat, add the onions and cook until soft. Add the flour, stir into
the fat and then gradually add about half the quantity of liquid. As this
soup is not going to cook for as long as the first one, a little more than
half the liquid will be enough. Add all the remaining ingredients and
cook gently for 1 to 1$\frac{1}{2}$ hours.

### GREEN BEAN SOUP (*Zöldbab leves*)   Hungary

6 servings:
$\frac{1}{2}$lb ($\frac{1}{4}$kg, $\frac{1}{2}$lb) green beans
4pt (2$\frac{1}{4}$l,5pt) stock or water
salt, pepper to taste
1oz (30g,2tb) butter
1 small onion, peeled and finely chopped
1oz (30g,$\frac{1}{4}$cup) flour
parsley, finely chopped
1tb lemon juice, strained
$\frac{1}{4}$pt (1dl,$\frac{2}{3}$cup) cream
mint or dill, chopped, to garnish

Wash, trim and slice the beans and cook until tender in the stock or
water. Add salt. In another large pan heat the butter, add the onion and

fry gently until soft. Add flour, mix well and, stirring all the time, cook for 5 to 10 minutes to bring out the full, slightly nutty flavour of flour and butter. Add the parsley. Strain the beans, put aside but keep the liquid. Gradually pour the bean liquid into the onion and flour mixture, stir and cook gently until the soup is thick. Add the beans, salt, pepper and lemon juice and cook for another 5 minutes. Just before serving, add the cream, stir well and serve. Sprinkle each bowl of soup with mint or dill.

## CABBAGE SOUP (*Krautersuppe*)   Austria

6 servings:
1 firm white cabbage
1oz (30g,2tb) butter or other fat
1oz (30g,$\frac{3}{4}$cup) flour
4pt (2$\frac{1}{4}$l,5pt) stock or water
salt, pepper to taste

Wash the cabbage and discard any broken leaves. Cut away the tough hard stalk. Cut into quarters, and shred. Put aside a handful of shredded leaves. Heat the fat in a large pan, add the cabbage and fry until it begins to brown, stirring it frequently to prevent burning and ensure even cooking. Add flour, stir well and continue cooking until the flour begins to brown. In another pan, bring the stock or water to the boil, then add this gradually to the cabbage, stirring all the time to avoid lumps forming. Add salt and pepper and cook gently for about 1 hour.

Just before serving, add the reserved cabbage as a garnish, making sure it is quite dry. If preferred, an egg yolk can be beaten into 1 to 2 tablespoons of cream, milk or water and then stirred into the soup immediately before serving.

This soup can be served with sliced fried German or Austrian-style sausages, with croûtons (see page 43) or triangles of fried bread.

Savoy cabbage is also cooked in the above style and fat bacon rinds are fried with the cabbage in the fat.

## CAULIFLOWER SOUP (*Karfiolsuppe*)   Austria

4–6 servings:
1 medium-sized cauliflower
1½oz (45g,3tb) butter
1½oz (45g,6tb) flour
salt, pepper and nutmeg to taste
1 egg yolk
3tb (4tb) milk or cream
grated cheese or garnish (optional)

Wash the cauliflower, discard any tough stalks or bruised leaves and break the cauliflower into 2 to 3 pieces. Cook in plenty of boiling salted water until tender but be careful it does not break up. Keeping the liquid gently boiling, take cauliflower from the pan with a perforated spoon, drain and break into flowerets. Put aside a few to be used later as a garnish. Mash the remainder or pass through a coarse sieve.

In another pan heat the butter, add the flour and stir to a roux. Little by little, add 1 cupful of the cauliflower liquid, stirring well. Return this to the rest of the cauliflower liquid, stirring all the time. Add salt, pepper, nutmeg and the sieved cauliflower. Beat the egg yolk into the milk. Take the pan from the stove, add the beaten egg mixture, whisk it lightly into the soup then return to the stove and let it cook gently, without boiling, for 2 to 3 minutes. Add the reserved cauliflower sprigs and serve a bowl of grated cheese separately.

## MUSHROOM SOUP (*Pilzsuppe*)   Austria

6 servings:
1lb (½kg,1lb) mushrooms
1½oz (45g,3tb) butter or other fat
1tb (1¼tb) parsley, finely chopped
1½oz (45g,6tb) flour
4pt (2¼l,5pt) clear stock
1tb (1¼tb) lemon juice, strained
salt to taste        1 egg yolk

Wash the mushrooms and slice thinly, stalks as well. Heat the butter or fat, add the parsley, stir well then add the mushrooms. Cook for 10 minutes, sprinkle with flour, stir again, add the stock stirring all the time and cook until mushrooms are tender. Add lemon juice and salt. Beat the egg yolk with a tablespoon of warm water, stir into the soup, whisk briskly and serve. Garnish with small semolina dumplings (see page 132).

## SAUERKRAUT SOUP (*Korhely leves*)   Hungary

The translation of the name of this soup is 'dissipated soup' and considered a great pick-me-up. It was one of the traditional dishes served in Hungary in the early hours of the morning after a night of dancing, drinking or gambling.

4–6 servings:

1lb ($\frac{1}{2}$kg,1lb) sauerkraut

4pt (2$\frac{1}{4}$l,5pt) water

1oz (30g,2tb) lard or other fat

1 small onion, peeled and finely chopped

1oz (30g,2tb) flour

1lb ($\frac{1}{2}$kg,1lb) smoked Debreciner sausages

salt to taste      2tsp paprika pepper

$\frac{1}{2}$tsp caraway seeds

$\frac{1}{2}$gill ($\frac{1}{2}$dl,$\frac{1}{3}$cup) sour cream or yogurt

Squeeze liquid from the sauerkraut and put sauerkraut aside. Dilute liquid with about the same quantity of the water. Put into a pan and bring to the boil.

Heat the fat in another large pan, add the onion and cook until soft. Add the flour, stir it into the fat but do not let it brown. Gradually add the remaining water, stirring all the time. Add the sauerkraut liquid and cook gently. Skin and slice the sausages and add to the pan. Add salt, paprika, caraway seeds and finally the sauerkraut. Stir well and cook over a gentle heat for 1 hour. Just before serving, add the sour cream.

This is almost a meal in itself. If Debreciner sausages are not available, use another type of smoked sausage from your delicatessen.

## TOMATO SOUP (*Paradiesersuppn*)   Bavaria

6 servings:
¾lb (375g,¾lb) tomatoes
1 small onion
1½oz (45g,3tb) fat
1½oz (45g,3tb) flour
salt, pepper to taste      1tsp sugar
3pt (1¾l,4pt) stock, or water
¼pt (1dl,⅔cup) sour cream
parsley, finely chopped, to garnish

Peel the tomatoes and chop into small pieces. Peel and finely chop the onion. Heat the fat in a large pan, add the onion and cook gently until it begins to change colour. Add tomatoes, stir well into fat, cover the pan and cook gently for 30 minutes. Sprinkle with flour, stir well, add salt, pepper and sugar. Little by little add the stock or water, stirring gently all the time until the soup is thick. Continue to cook over a moderate heat for 10 minutes until the soup is gently boiling. Add sour cream, stir and take at once from the stove. Serve sprinkled lightly with parsley.

## POTATO (GARLIC) SOUP (*Česneková Polévka*)   Czechoslovakia

4–6 servings:
1½lb (¾kg,1½lb) large potatoes
salt, pepper to taste
¼pt (1dl,⅔cup) milk      1 egg yolk
1oz (30g,2tb) butter
garlic cloves

Wash, peel and chop the potatoes. Cook in plenty of boiling, salted water until soft. Rub the potatoes and their liquid through a coarse sieve and return to the pan. Beat the milk with the egg yolk, stir this into the sieved potatoes, add the butter, test for seasoning and bring gently to the boil. Flavour generously with pepper. Peel the garlic, crush it and divide between 4 to 6 soup plates. Pour the hot soup over the top and serve.

## POTATO SOUP (*Kartoffelsuppe*)    Austria

4–6 servings:
1lb (½kg,1lb) potatoes
1 celery stalk, chopped
1 carrot, coarsely chopped
salt, pepper to taste
1½oz (45g,3tb) fat
1 onion, finely chopped
1oz (30g,¼cup) flour
1tsp (1¼tsp) lemon peel, grated
½tsp (¾tsp) caraway seeds
¼tsp (½tsp) dried marjoram
parsley, finely chopped, to garnish

Wash and peel the potatoes and chop into small pieces. Put into a pan with plenty of water, celery stalk and carrot. Add salt. Cook until vegetables are soft. Heat fat in another pan, add the onion and simmer until it browns. Add the flour, stir it into the fat to make a roux then gradually add 1 cupful of the potato liquid, stirring all the time. Add the lemon peel, caraway seeds and marjoram. Now add this to the potatoes and stir well. Just before serving, add pepper to taste and sprinkle with parsley.

## BOHEMIAN OUKROP (*Staročeský*)    Czechoslovakia

This is a peasant dish and the ingredients are rather as available.

6 servings:
4–6 small cloves garlic
salt, pepper to taste
½lb (250g,½lb) potatoes
4pt (2¼l,5pt) water
½tsp (¾tsp) caraway seeds

¼tsp (½tsp) dried marjoram
¼tsp (½tsp) ground ginger (optional)
1oz (30g,2tb) lard or shortening
6 slices rye bread
fat for frying bread

Crush garlic and mash until smooth with a little salt. Peel and chop the potatoes. Put the water into a large pan, add the garlic, potatoes, caraway seeds, marjoram and ginger, if using. Finally add the measured quantity of fat and cook all together over a moderate heat until the potatoes are soft. Test for seasoning and add salt and pepper if required.

While the soup is cooking, cut the bread into small chunks. Heat enough fat to fry these until brown and crisp—this is the *oukrop*. Divide these into 6 bowls, add the hot soup and serve when the bread has been well soaked—about a minute.

### PEASANT SOUP (*Paraszt Gulyàs leves*)   Hungary

6–8 servings:
1 large onion
1½oz (45g,3tb) fat
1tsp paprika pepper
1 garlic clove, crushed
4pt (2¼l,5pt) water, warm
salt to taste
2lb (1kg,2lb) potatoes
½lb (¼kg,½lb) tomatoes
1–2 sweet peppers
½tsp (¾tsp) caraway seeds

Peel and chop the onion. Heat the fat in a large pan, add the onion and cook it gently until it changes colour. Add the paprika pepper and stir well. Add the garlic and the warm water. Bring to the boil, add the salt. Peel the potatoes and cut into small cubes. Add to the pan. Peel and chop the tomatoes, cut the peppers into thin strips, discarding the core and seeds, and sprinkle with caraway seeds. Add to the soup. Stir, cover, continue cooking until the potatoes are soft, and serve.

## BEGGARS' SOUP (*Bettelmannssuppe*)   Austria

6 servings:
6 slices rye bread
butter, for spreading
4pt (2¼l, 5pt) stock
salt, pepper to taste
6 eggs
parsley, finely chopped, to garnish

Toast the bread and spread generously with butter. Cut into cubes and divide into 6 soup bowls. Bring the stock to the boil. Add salt and pepper. Break 1 egg into each bowl and sprinkle with parsley. Pour boiling stock into each bowl and serve at once.

Unless the stock is absolutely boiling the eggs will not cook, so return the pan to the stove between each serving to make sure.

## CHEESE SOUP (*Käsesuppe*)   Austria

6 servings:
2oz (60g, ⅔cup) grated hard cheese
3 bread rolls
2oz (60g, 4tb) butter or other fat
3pt (1⅔l, 4pt) clear stock
1 egg yolk
¼pt (1dl, ⅔cup) milk or cream

Instead of bread rolls, fairly thick sliced bread may be used. Remove crust and cut bread into small cubes. Heat the butter, add the bread cubes and fry until brown and crisp. Put the stock into a large pan, bring gently to the boil, add the bread cubes and mix well into the stock. Add the cheese, stir well. Beat the egg yolk into the milk and stir this swiftly into the simmering soup. Do not let the soup cook further and serve immediately.

If the bread is correctly fried it will swell but still retain its shape.

## SEMOLINA SOUP (*Geröstete Griessuppn*)    Bavaria

6 servings:
4oz (125g,1cup) coarse semolina
2oz (60g,4tb) fat
4pt (2¼l,5pt) stock or water
salt, pepper, nutmeg to taste
chives, finely chopped to taste

Heat the fat in a large pan, add the semolina and fry it, stirring all the time until it turns golden. Add the liquid, stir well and cook over a moderate heat for 20 to 25 minutes. Just before serving, add the salt, pepper, nutmeg and chives.

This is also a popular Austrian soup. Sometimes just before serving, a well-beaten egg is stirred into the soup and fairly large croûtons are offered separately as a garnish.

Note:—It is important to use coarse semolina.

## FISH SOUP OR STEW (*Bogràcsos hal* or *Szegedi halàszlè*)    Hungary

This is a typical fish soup or stew similar to those made in other parts of Europe but using freshwater fish. Among the varieties considered essential are carp, bass and sterlet.

The fish is cleaned, scaled and cut into rather large slices. Really small fish are placed whole at the bottom of an earthenware pot, called *bogràcs*, followed by alternate layers of large pieces of fish and peeled, sliced onion. The finest pieces of fish, usually the sterlet, are placed on top. Salt, paprika pepper and just enough water to cover are added. It is brought to the boil and cooked over a moderate heat for at least 30 to 40 minutes. The pan is gently shaken from time to time but the contents must not be stirred. The soup is served from the dish in which it was cooked, the fish taken out with a perforated spoon, and over each portion is poured some of the broth.

## FISH SOUP (*Halleves*)  Hungary

When buying the fish for this recipe, ask for some fish heads and trimmings for the fish stock. Most fishmongers are willing to give or sell these cheaply.

4–6 servings:
2pt (1l,2½pt) fish stock
1 each of small carrot, red onion, turnip
1 each stalk celery, large potato
1pt (½l,1¼pt) water
2tb lemon juice
salt, pepper to taste
1½oz (45g,3tb) lard, shortening or other fat
1½oz (45g,6tb) flour
½pt (¼l,1¼cups) dry white wine or beer
½lb (250g,½lb) white fish, cooked and flaked

Put the fish heads and trimmings into a large pan, add enough water to make the required quantity of stock and cook for 20 to 30 minutes. While the stock is cooking, wash, peel or scrape and grate the vegetables. Put these with the water into another pan, add the lemon juice, salt and pepper and cook gently until soft.

Strain the fish stock and put aside. Rub the vegetables with their liquid through a coarse sieve. Heat the fat in a large pan, add the flour and stir to a roux. Little by little add the fish stock, stirring all the time until it thickens.

Add the vegetables with their liquid, stirring all the time. Add the wine or beer, stir again and add the cooked, flaked fish. Bring slowly to the boil, stirring gently and simmer for about 5 minutes. Serve at once.

Instead of white fish, cooked or frozen shrimps or small prawns may be used.

## CHILLED APPLE SOUP (*Apfelsuppe*)  Austria

4 servings:
½lb (¼kg,½lb) apples
1 thick slice lemon
1  small piece  cinnamon
1pt (½l,2½cups) water
2oz (60g,4tb) sugar
1 egg yolk
wine biscuits (cookies) for serving

Peel, core and slice the apples. Put into a pan with the lemon, cinnamon and water. Cook gently until very soft. Rub through a sieve, return to the pan and add the sugar. Beat egg yolk into 2 or 3 tablespoons warm water and add to the soup, stirring all the time. Cool, chill and serve in deep glass bowls with wine biscuits or rusks.

## CHILLED APRICOT SOUP (*Aprikosen-Kaltschale*)  Austria

4 servings:
½lb (¼kg,½lb) fresh apricots
1pt (½l,1¼pt) white wine
2oz (60g,¼cup) sugar
1tb lemon juice
wine biscuits (cookies) for serving

Put aside 2 or 3 apricots, stone them and thinly slice. Stone and coarsely chop the rest and purée in a liquidiser together with the wine, sugar and lemon juice. Chill until required.

Serve very cold in small, deep glass bowls, garnish with the sliced apricots and serve sweet wine biscuits as an accompaniment.

## WINE SOUP WITH BROTH AND CREAM (*Terlaner Weinsuppe*)
### Austria

4 servings:
½pt (¼l,1¼cups) dry white wine
4 egg yolks
½pt (¼l,1¼cups) thick heavy cream
1pt (½l,2½cups) clear stock (see recipe for Boiled Beef, page 73)
ryebread croûtons to garnish

Beat the 4 egg yolks until smooth then combine with the remaining ingredients. Mix well and cook gently in a thick pan on top of the stove until the mixture is thick and creamy.

Croûtons (see page 43) made from black or very dark brown bread and sprinkled with cinnamon are served separately with this soup.

# SOUP GARNISHES

There are no boundaries for these. Throughout Central Europe soup is an everyday food and stock always available. The stock generally is not especially refined unless for a special occasion and is usually made from the bones and left-overs of the week's cooking. These stocks are often used as a broth and varied by the use of different garnishings.

The following garnishes are used throughout Central Europe.

## CROÛTONS

These are small cubes or squares of bread which have been browned by frying or baking. They can be used immediately or stored in a closed container and kept in a cool, dry place for at least 2 weeks.

sliced bread
fat for frying (shallow)

Cut off the bread crusts and cut the slices into small cubes, not too small or they become like small bullets when fried. Have a pan ready with a little hot butter, oil or other fat, but not dripping as the flavour is too strong. Fry the cubes quickly, stirring all the time to ensure even cooking and no burning. When they are crisp and a golden brown, they are ready.

## SCHOEBERL (*Schoeberl*)    Austria

These are a typical Austrian addition to a clear soup. They are light and airy, a little like a custard and quite simple to prepare. Usually they are baked in a special tin (*Schoeberlpfanne*) in the oven, allowed to cool, cut into squares or small triangles, then reheated in the oven just before serving. They can be cooked in any type of baking pan, although a square or oblong pan makes for easier cutting.

4–6 servings:
2 eggs
pinch of salt
2oz (60g,½cup) flour
butter to grease pan

Separate the egg yolks from the whites. Whisk the whites with a pinch of salt until very stiff. Beat the yolks until smooth. Combine the yolks and whites, then fold in the flour. Butter a baking pan, sprinkle with flour and pour in the batter. Bake in a moderate oven (350°F: 180°C: Gas 4) for about 15 minutes or until it rises and is a golden brown. Take from the oven and cool. Cut into squares, strips or triangles and serve separately on a warm plate or drop at the very last moment into a clear soup before serving.

## EGG BATTER STRANDS (*Eingetröpftes*)    Austria

4–6 servings:
2 eggs, well beaten
2oz (60g,½cup) flour
pinch of salt

Mix the flour into the eggs, adding salt, and beat to a smooth batter. The exact quantity of flour depends on the size of the eggs. The batter must be thick but of a pouring consistency. Have ready a pan of boiling stock. Pour the batter through a large funnel into the boiling stock, moving it in circles. Leave to rise once, then take the pan from the heat and serve.

SHREDDED PANCAKES (*Tiroler Fridattene* or *Fridattene*)   Austria

These are thin unsweetened pancakes which are rolled, cooled and cut into thin strips. The strips are added to the soup just before serving. Plain omelettes are treated in the same manner.

'BAKER'S PEAS' (*Backerbsen*)   Austria

I am somewhat at a loss for a good translation of these excellent little additions served with clear soups. These have nothing to do with peas but are small balls of fried batter which are either added to clear soups immediately before serving, or served separately.

4–6 servings:

2oz (60g, 2½tb) plain flour

1 egg

2tb (2½tb) milk or water

salt to taste

oil, or fat, for frying

Put the flour into a bowl, add the egg and beat until the mixture is smooth. Add the liquid; the mixture must be thick but of a running consistency. Beat well and add salt. Heat about ¾ to 1 inch of oil or fat in a large frying pan.

Pour the batter through a sieve with very large holes or through a perforated spoon into the hot fat, about a ladleful at a time. As it drops into the fat it breaks up into small balls or 'peas.' As soon as the 'peas' are a golden brown, take them out and drain on absorbent paper.

This operation of pouring the batter through the sieve does require a little explanation.

In Austria they use a sieve with extra large holes through which they pour the batter into the fat. But a perforated spoon does quite well. As you pour the batter through the spoon or sieve, move it over the fat to make sure the batter is dispersed. Do not try to pour all of the batter into the fat at one time or the batter will stick like a pancake.

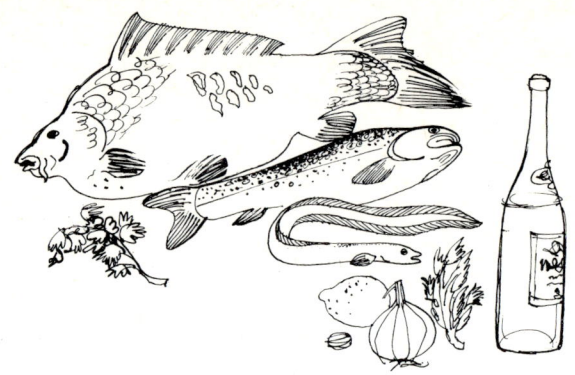

# FISH

### CARP (*Kapr*)   Czechoslovakia

This is a Christmas dish. Some cooks call it black carp, others devilled carp. Identical dishes are prepared by the Silesians, the Austrians, Poles and other nationalities in this region.

Carp are said to have been originally brought to Europe centuries ago from China and are a favourite Central European and Jewish dish. Carp can be bought whole or cut into pieces. They must be carefully washed in salted water and then in vinegar and water mixed, although some cooks wash them once more in undiluted vinegar. When washing a whole fish, be careful to remove the spleen which lies behind the head. For the following recipe the blood must be kept.

4–6 servings:
3lb (1¼kg,3lb) carp
2tb (2½tb) vinegar
1 carrot
1 small piece each hamburger parsley and celeriac
1 onion, small
2oz (60g,4tb) butter or fat
¾pt (⅓l,2cups) water or brown ale
6 peppercorns      salt to taste

46

pinch of allspice
1 bay leaf      pinch of thyme
½tsp ground ginger
2 strips lemon rind
¼lb (125g,¼lb) gingerbread, grated
2tb (2½tb) redcurrant jelly
1oz (30g,¼cup) white flour
2tsp brown sugar
¼pt (1dl, ⅔cup) red wine
a few prunes, nuts and raisins to garnish

The flavour of carp is considered much improved if prepared the day before it is required. It must be reheated for serving.

Remove the scales and clean the carp thoroughly (keep a few scales from the carp in your purse; this indicates money the whole year through, say the Germans). Put the blood from the carp aside and dilute this with a little vinegar. Rub the fish inside and out with remaining vinegar. Flatten the fish and put aside.

Clean the root vegetables and cut into rounds. Peel and thinly slice the onion. Heat half the butter in a large pan, add the onion and fry gently until golden brown. Add about 2 cupfuls of water (or brown ale if preferred), the diluted blood, peppercorns, salt, allspice, herbs, ginger and 1 strip of lemon rind. Stir well and bring gently to the boil. Cook for 10 minutes, then add the gingerbread, redcurrant jelly and the prepared carp. Cover and continue cooking gently but steadily.

In another small pan heat the remaining butter, add the flour, fry and stir to a dark brown roux. Add half the brown sugar. Mix well, then add enough hot water to dilute the roux to a thin paste. Lift the fish from its pan, put aside but keep warm. Pour the roux into the pan in which the fish was cooking and, stirring well into the sauce, continue cooking for 5 minutes. Strain the sauce through a fine sieve and return it to the pan. Add the fish, 1 strip of lemon rind, a few stoned and chopped prunes, nuts and raisins, sprinkle lightly with the remaining brown sugar and add the red wine. Continue cooking for 10 minutes or until the carp is tender, and the head fin can be easily pulled off. Take the carp from the pan, place in a shallow dish, cover with the sauce and leave until next day.

Serve with plain boiled potatoes.

## BAKED CARP (*Ponty vajban*)   Hungary

Instead of carp, almost any firm white fish can be used for this recipe.

4–6 servings:
one whole carp,  $2\frac{1}{2}$–3lb ($1$–$1\frac{1}{4}$kg,$2\frac{1}{2}$–3lb)
4 potatoes
salt to taste
3oz (90g,6tb) butter
$\frac{1}{2}$pt ($\frac{1}{4}$l,$1\frac{1}{4}$cups) fresh cream

Wash and parboil the potatoes. Cool, peel and cut into medium-thick slices. Clean, scale and wipe the carp with a wet cloth. Make a few incisions along the edges and sprinkle the fish lightly with salt. Rub the bottom of an oval baking dish with some of the butter then cover with a thick layer of potatoes. Place the fish on top, pour the cream over the fish. Cut the remaining butter into slivers and sprinkle these over the top. Bake in a moderate oven (350°F: 180°C: Gas 4) for about 30 minutes, basting frequently.

When the fish is cooked, serve hot in the dish in which it was baked.

There are slight variations to this dish. Sometimes the fish is baked in the oven with the potatoes, generously sprinkled with slivers of butter, for 15 to 20 minutes before the cream is added. In some recipes the cream is mixed with about 1 tablespoon of paprika pepper. Another version spreads thinly sliced peeled tomatoes and green peppers over the fish before baking, and adds cream just before serving.

## EEL IN WINE WITH CREAM SAUCE (*Aal auf Feinschmeckerart*)
### Austria

4–6 servings:
1lb (½kg,1lb) eel
salt, pepper to taste
a few mixed root vegetables (see method)
1 onion
1tb vinegar or lemon juice
½pt (¼l,1¼cups) white wine, or wine and water
1 cup cream sauce (see method)
lemon wedges and croûtons to garnish

Ask the fishmonger to skin the eel for you—ideally this should be done while it is still alive. Cut the eel into 10 pieces, sprinkle lightly with salt and leave for 30 minutes.

Prepare the mixed vegetables (ie 1 each carrot, parsnip, celery or turnip, it depends on the season) and cut into rounds. Peel and slice the onion. Spread the vegetables on the bottom of a shallow pan, add the eel, salt, pepper, vinegar and white wine or a mixture of white wine and water to cover. Bring gently just to the boil, then lower the heat and cook gently until the eel is tender, 30 to 45 minutes, but much depends on its thickness.

While the eel is cooking, make the sauce. This is simply a thick white or béchamel sauce to which 3 or 4 tablespoons of rich (heavy) cream is added. Keep warm. Lift the eel pieces from the pan with a fish slice. Take out the bones and place the flesh on a warmed dish. Pour the sauce over the eel and serve with triangles of fried bread and wedges of lemon.

Eels also are cooked in the same way in red wine.

## FRESH HERRINGS IN PARSLEY SAUCE (*Grüne Heringe in Krautersosse*)   Austria

The interest the Viennese take in herrings is perhaps curious. All Austrians love their carnivals, and the old-time *Fasching* not only brought love, life and gaiety but also some pretty crashing hangovers. So on Ash Wednesday all anyone could eat was marinated herrings, and they are now considered good for a hangover. At one time marinated herrings were imported from Russia and there is one variety of herring still known as Russian.

Sometime during the last century, some restaurateurs organised another festival, the *Heringsschmaus* or Herring Feast, thus extending the fun and games for another day. But the *Heringsschmaus* is no longer with us and even *Fasching*, alas, is not what it was.

For this recipe you need fresh herrings and warm parsley sauce. Quantities are as required but there must be enough sauce to cover the herrings.

The herrings must be cleaned, their heads removed but otherwise left whole. Put them into a pan, cover with parsley sauce (thick white sauce to which chopped, fresh parsley has been added, to taste) and cook gently until tender. Serve with boiled potatoes or boiled rice.

## FRESH HERRINGS WITH A HORSERADISH SAUCE
### (*Grüne Heringe mit Krensosse*)   Austria

herrings
horseradish sauce (see page 126)

Clean the herrings, cut off the heads but keep the fish whole. Cook them in water with a little chopped onion, salt, pepper and chopped parsley until tender. Drain well and serve with a bowl of horseradish sauce and plain boiled potatoes, sprinkled lightly with finely chopped parsley.

## HERRINGS WITH A CREAM AND ANCHOVY SAUCE
### (*Grüne Heringe in Rahmsosse*)   Austria

4–6 servings:
4–6 fresh (green) herrings, filleted
1oz (30g, 2tb) butter or other fat
¼pt (1dl⅔cup) sour cream or yogurt
fine breadcrumbs
salt, pepper to taste
4–6 anchovy fillets

Rub a baking dish with half the butter. Place the herring fillets on the bottom. Cover with sour cream or yogurt and spread thickly with breadcrumbs.

Sprinkle with salt and pepper and lay 1 anchovy fillet along the top of each herring fillet. Dot with slivers of the remaining butter and bake in a moderate oven (350°F: 180°C: Gas 4) for 30 minutes.


## BAKED HERRINGS (*Heringe vom Rost*)   Austria

6 servings:
6 fresh herrings
salt to taste
1oz (30g,2tb) melted butter
juice of $\frac{1}{2}$ lemon
chopped parsley, to garnish

Clean the herrings, wash the cavities, sprinkle the fish lightly with salt and rub with melted butter. Place in a shallow baking pan and bake in a moderate oven (350°F: 180°C: Gas 4) until tender, 10 to 12 minutes. Sprinkle with lemon juice and parsley just before serving.

Serve hot with plain boiled potatoes or a green salad, or chilled with *maître d'hôtel* butter.

To make this, beat some chopped fresh parsley into unsalted butter, add a few drops of lemon juice and a little salt and pepper to taste.


## FOGAS 'MILLER'S WIFE' STYLE (*Fogas molnàrnè mòdra*) Hungary

6 servings:
3lb (1½kg,3lb) fogas or pike
salt, pepper to taste
flour for dusting
oil for frying
3oz (90g,6tb) butter or other fat
parsley, coarsely chopped, to garnish
lemon wedges, to garnish

Wash, clean and skin the fish and cut into thick slices. Sprinkle lightly with salt and pepper and roll in flour. In a large pan heat enough oil for shallow frying and fry the fish slices on both sides until golden in colour. Meanwhile, melt the butter in a small pan.

Serve the fish on a hot plate. Pour the hot, melted butter over the top and sprinkle generously with parsley. Garnish with wedges of lemon and serve at once.

Fresh haddock can be cooked in the same manner.


## FOGAS ROBIN HOOD STYLE (*Fogas betyàr mòdra*)   Hungary

6 servings:
3lb (1½kg) fogas or pike
½lb (¼kg) mushrooms
2½oz (70g, 5tb) butter or other fat
salt to taste
1 large onion, peeled and finely chopped
2tsp paprika pepper
1tb (heaped) flour
1pt (½l, 2½cups) sour cream
parsley, chopped, to garnish

Wash, fillet and skin the fish. Wash and thinly slice the mushrooms. Rub a shallow baking dish with butter and arrange the fish fillets in it. Put aside. Cook the fish head, bones and skin in lightly salted water. Heat the rest of the butter in a frying pan and fry the onion. Add the mushrooms, cook these for about 5 minutes, then stir in the paprika pepper. Strain off the fish liquid, pour this into the onion-mushroom mixture and stir gently. Continue simmering. Mix the flour into the sour cream, stir this into the pan and bring gently to the boil, stirring all the time. Pour this sauce at once over the fish fillets and put into a moderate oven (350°F: 180°C: Gas 4). Bake until tender, 15 to 20 minutes.

Garnish with parsley and serve with plain boiled potatoes.

Almost any firm white fish can be cooked in the above manner, in particular fresh filleted haddock. Usually a fishmonger will clean, skin and fillet fish if asked.

The *betyàrs* were outlaws of the Robin Hood variety robbing the rich and assisting the poor. They were a mixed band, some peasants avoiding military service, others fighting oppression, etc. They were in existence even as late as the nineteenth century, and many are the legends and songs recording their exploits.

## BLUE TROUT (*Forellen Blau Gekocht*)  Austria

6 servings:
6 trout
salt to taste
1 clove
2 peppercorns
few drops lemon juice
white wine or tarragon vinegar to cover (for method 2 only)
parsley, coarsely chopped, to garnish

There are several ways of cooking trout 'blue' and other fresh small fish can be cooked in the same way, for example small pike and fresh herrings. The most important point is that the fish must be absolutely fresh, preferably still alive when they meet their fate in the kitchen.

There is some local argument as to whether trout cooked 'blue' requires the somewhat heavy flavour of vinegar. If the fish is absolutely fresh, then follow method 1; if fresh but not actually alive, use method 2.

**Method 1**

Kill the fish with a smart blow on the back of the head. Do not wash or rub with salt but clean carefully through the gills, handling the fish as little as possible. (It is the slime on the fish which, when cooked, gives it the coveted blue sheen.)

Bring to the boil enough very lightly salted water to cover the fish, adding the clove, peppercorns and lemon juice. If liked, a few thin strips of onion may be added as well. Add the fish and continue simmering but so gently that no bubbles disturb the surface of the liquid. Leave for 8 to 10 minutes, depending on the size of the fish. Small pike require a few minutes longer than trout but remember trout must always be well cooked so that the flesh comes away easily from the bones when eaten.

When the fish are tender, take them gently from the pan, place side by side on a warmed platter and cover with a napkin. Serve hot, accompanied with boiled potatoes, a dish of melted butter and coarsely chopped parsley, or cold with a French dressing flavoured lightly with capers, a sauce tartare, or mayonnaise.

## Method 2

Clean fish as for method 1 and, when prepared for cooking, place them side by side in a shallow pan and cover with wine or mild vinegar. Bring gently to the boil, take the pan from the stove and leave for ½ minute. Take from the pan and drop each fish into ice-cold water. Take out immediately and place them on a plate spaced well apart. Some experts insist they are placed in a draught to help obtain the blue sheen. Slip them carefully into a boiling *court bouillon* or hot water to which has been added 5 tablespoons each of white wine and vinegar, plus the seasoning. Take the pan from the stove, cover the fish and leave for 10 to 12 minutes, depending on the size of the fish. To test whether the fish are ready, pull at the fins: if they appear to come away easily, the fish is ready. Serve as above.

### TROUT IN WHITE WINE (*Forellen in Weinsosse*)   Austria

4 servings:
4 trout
½pt (¼l,1¼cups) dry white wine
4 peppercorns
½ small onion, peeled and chopped
parsley, chopped to garnish
thyme to taste
1oz (30g,2tb) butter or other fat
½oz (15g,2tb) flour
lemon wedges to garnish

Clean the trout as instructed in the previous recipe. Put the fish with the wine, peppercorns, onion, parsley and thyme into a shallow pan, bring gently to the boil and cook with the liquid just trembling until the trout are tender, about 8 minutes. Take from the pan, remove the eyes and place the fish on a warm dish. Put aside but keep warm. Strain the stock.

While the fish are cooking, melt the butter in another pan, add the flour and stir to a roux. Gradually add the fish stock, stir and cook gently for 10 minutes. Pour this sauce over the fish and serve with wedges of lemon and boiled potatoes.

## FISH CUTLETS IN MUSTARD SAUCE (*Hecht in Senfsosse*)   Austria

The original recipe calls for pike but other thick, firm white cutlets may be cooked in the same way.

4–6 servings:
4–6 firm fish cutlets
salt to taste
lard or other fat, for frying
continental mustard, for spreading
a few capers (optional)
lemon wedges to garnish

Wipe the fish with a damp cloth, put into a bowl and sprinkle with salt. Leave for 1 hour. Wipe dry. Heat enough fat in a frying pan to fry all the cutlets at the same time. Spread each cutlet generously on both sides with mustard (it must be continental mustard, English mustard is far too strong for this dish). Fry the cutlets first on one side until brown, then turn and fry the other side. Lower the heat and let the fish cook very gently until tender, basting from time to time.   A few capers can be added to the fish after it has been browned.

Serve with lemon wedges and boiled potatoes.

Any of the mild continental mustards can be used in the above recipe. I favour a rather aromatic French mustard if I am cooking a mild-flavoured fish, but a German one for a strongly flavoured fish. It is a particularly good way of dressing up a piece of lesser-quality fish.

## PAPRIKA FISH WITH RED WINE (*Fisch-Paprikasch mit Rotwein*)
Austria

Since most people think of fish and white wine, this recipe might seem something of an oddity. Usually it is prepared with carp and sturgeon combined, 2lb of the former to 1lb of the latter. However, other firm fish such as cod and hake can be used in the same manner.

6 servings:
2lb (1kg,2lb) carp
1lb (½kg,1lb) sturgeon
salt to taste
1½oz (45g,3tb) butter or other fat
1 large onion, peeled and finely sliced
1tb paprika pepper
red wine to cover

Clean the fish and cut into small portions; remove as many bones as possible. Sprinkle lightly with salt. Heat the butter in a large shallow pan, add the onion and gently fry until golden brown. Stir in paprika, add the fish and enough red wine to cover. Cover the pan and cook over a good heat until the fish is tender, about 20 minutes but the exact time depends on the fish used. Test from time to time, or the fish might overcook.

To serve, take out the fish, place it on a warmed plate and cover with the onion and wine sauce. Boiled potatoes are the usual accompaniment.

## BAKED PAPRIKA FISH (*Paprika Fisch*)    Austria

6 servings:
3lb (1½kg,3lb) freshwater fish
salt, pepper to taste
1oz (30g,2tb) butter or other fat
1 large onion, peeled and chopped
1tb paprika pepper
½pt (¼l,1¼cups) cream
lemon wedges to garnish

The fish can be cooked whole, in thick steaks or in fillets.

Clean and wash the fish and rub with salt and pepper. Heat the butter in a large baking pan, add the onion and cook gently until golden brown. Place the fish on top, sprinkle with paprika and pour the cream over the top. Bake in a moderate oven (350°F: 180°C: Gas 4) for about 30 minutes, basting frequently. Whole fish may take longer, between 35 to 40 minutes, while steaks and fillets take between 20 to 25 minutes.

Lift the fish from the pan with a fish slice and place on a hot serving dish. Pour the sauce over the top.

Serve with boiled potatoes and wedges of lemon.


FISH AND POTATO CASSEROLE (*Halas burgonya*)    Hungary

4–6 servings:
2lb (1kg,2lb) fish fillets
2lb (1kg,2lb) floury potatoes
salt, pepper to taste
$\frac{1}{2}$ cup butter or other fat
$\frac{1}{2}$ small onion, peeled and finely chopped
4tb (5tb) hot milk
1tb paprika pepper
$\frac{1}{2}$pt ($\frac{1}{4}$l,1$\frac{1}{4}$cups) fresh or sour cream
fine breadcrumbs, for sprinkling
paprika pepper and slivers of butter to garnish

Wash, peel and cut the potatoes in quarters. Cook in salted water until soft. While the potatoes are cooking, wipe the fish with a damp cloth. Sprinkle lightly with salt and pepper. Heat two-thirds of the butter in a shallow pan, add the fillets and simmer them until brown on both sides and tender enough to flake. Take from the pan, separate into flakes and put aside. In the same fat, fry the onion until soft and golden brown.

Drain the potatoes and mash until very smooth. Add the rest of the butter and, when thoroughly mixed into the potatoes, add enough hot milk to make the mixture smooth and fluffy. Season with salt, pepper and paprika. Spread lightly on the bottom of a baking dish. Spread about one-third of the cream over the potatoes, add the onion and then a layer of breadcrumbs. Arrange the flaked fish on top. Sprinkle fairly generously with breadcrumbs, spread the remaining cream over the top, dot with slivers of butter, and sprinkle with paprika. Bake in a moderate oven (350°F: 180°C: Gas 4) for 20 to 30 minutes or until the potatoes are reheated and the butter melted into the crumbs.

Serve at once.

### FISH GRATIN (*Gratinierter Fisch Beliebiger Art*)   Austria

4–6 servings:
2lb (1kg,2lb) firm white fish, cooked
3oz (90g,6tb) butter or other fat
½lb (¼kg,½lb) potatoes
1pt (½l,1¼pt) milk, warmed
1oz (30g,¼cup) flour
grated cheese to taste
salt to taste
1–2 egg yolks well beaten
breadcrumbs for sprinkling

Flake the fish and make sure there are no bones left in it. Rub a baking dish with a little of the butter and add the fish. Wash and peel the potatoes and cook in boiling salted water until soft. Drain and rub through a potato ricer and mash; it is important there should be no lumps in the potatoes. Add one-third of the butter, beat this well into the potatoes and then add enough of the milk to make a thick creamy purée. Pipe through a large plain piping tube round the side of the dish. Heat another third of the butter, add the flour and cook, stirring all the time, to a roux. Gradually add enough of the remaining milk to make a medium-thick sauce. Add grated cheese and salt to taste and then take the pan from the heat and beat in the egg yolks. Pour this over the fish, but not over the potatoes, sprinkle with breadcrumbs and grated cheese and dot with the remaining butter cut into slivers. Bake in a fairly hot oven (400°F: 200°C: Gas 6) until the top is brown.

# POULTRY AND GAME

### POINTERS FOR POULTRY AND GAME

In the following recipes it is assumed that the poultry and game has been purchased, dressed and drawn, ready for the pot or oven.

If using frozen poultry, let it thaw at room temperature for as long as necessary—perhaps overnight. Chickens must be *completely* defrosted before using. They may contain salmonella, a toxic which only exists when the chicken is in its frozen state and which is rendered harmless when the chicken is completely thawed.

### VIENNESE FRIED CHICKEN (*Wiener Backhendl*)   Austria

2–4 servings:
1 young chicken
salt, pepper to taste
flour, for coating
1–2 eggs, well beaten
fine breadcrumbs for coating
pork fat or lard for deep frying

Cut the chicken neatly into 4 pieces. (In Vienna the poulterer does this and, perhaps to prove to his customers it is a chicken, he leaves the skinned head on one of the pieces.) Pull off the skin to make the coating stick more firmly.

Rub the chicken pieces lightly with salt and pepper, then coat with flour, dip into the beaten egg and finally into the breadcrumbs. Heat plenty of fat, there must be at least 1 inch of very hot fat in the pan. Carefully place the chicken pieces in the hot fat, fry them to a golden brown, then lower the heat to let the chicken pieces cook through without further browning —between 10 and 15 minutes. Drain the chicken pieces on absorbent paper.

Serve on a hot dish accompanied by a green salad, lemon wedges, fried parsley, sliced tomatoes and gherkins.

The liver and the stomach are usually cleaned, coated in flour, egg and breadcrumbs and fried in deep fat. As both take only a moment or so to fry, put them into the fat just before the chicken pieces are ready.

This method of cooking chicken is as Viennese as Vienna itself.

### PAPRIKA CHICKEN (*Csirke paprikàs*)   Hungary

6 servings:
2–3 spring chickens
3oz (90g,6tb) butter or other fat
3 medium-sized onions, peeled and thickly sliced
2 red sweet peppers, cored and quartered
1tb paprika pepper
2tb (2½tb) mild vinegar
salt, pepper to taste
stock or water, to cover
1½lb (¾kg,1½lb) small potatoes
3tb (4tb) sour cream

Heat a large pan, add the butter and lightly fry the onions without browning them. Add the sweet peppers and simmer them gently for a few minutes; add the paprika and vinegar, the chickens, salt and pepper and cook for 15 minutes. Add enough liquid to cover, cover the pan and cook the chickens over a moderate heat until tender. Wash and cook the potatoes until soft. Cool and peel.

Just before serving, add the sour cream and the potatoes to the chickens. Continue cooking for a few minutes. Take the chickens from the pan and cut each in half. Put these into a hot serving dish, add some of the sauce (serve the rest separately) and garnish with the onions, peppers and potatoes.

Serve with noodles or tiny dumplings (see page 130).

### CHICKEN STEW (*Csirke pörkölt*)   Hungary

*Pörkölt* is a stew flavoured with paprika pepper and a largish quantity of onions. All *pörkölts* are cooked in the same manner, whether prepared with meat, poultry or game. The word *pörkölt* literally means scorched or singed.

4–6 servings:

3lb (1½kg,3lb) chicken pieces

3oz (90g,6tb) lard or other fat

4 large onions, peeled and sliced

1tb paprika pepper

salt, pepper to taste

2–3 tomatoes

1–2 green peppers

Heat the lard and fry the onions until brown. Add the paprika pepper and stir it well into the onions. Add the chicken pieces and brown these well, bordering on being scorched, as the name suggests. Add salt and pepper and just enough water to prevent burning—this is not meant to be a stew with a lot of liquid. While the chicken is cooking, peel and chop the tomatoes; discard the core and seeds of the peppers and cut the flesh into strips. Add the peppers then the tomatoes to the pan, a little more water if required and continue cooking until the chicken is quite tender.

It is usual to serve *galuska* (see page 130) with a *pörkölt* and either toast and pickled cucumbers, or a green salad.

If using veal or pork, this must be cut into medium-sized cubes. This is an extremely useful recipe for small portions of poultry, ie the wings and legs.

## THE EMPEROR'S PULLET (*Csàszàr Jèrce*)   Hungary

Fattened pullets are a speciality of Hungary and weigh 4 to 5lb each.

6 servings:
4–5lb (2–2¼kg, 4–5lb) pullet
salt to taste
4oz (125g, ½cup) lard
¼pt (1dl, ⅔cup) cream
¼pt (1dl, ⅔cup) dry white wine
2tb each of extra white wine and cream

Cut the chicken into neat joints, place in a casserole and sprinkle lightly with salt. Heat the lard until very hot and pour this over the chicken pieces. Cook over a moderate heat until the chicken is a good brown all over. Turn the pieces from time to time and baste frequently with the hot fat.

Combine the first quantities of cream and wine. Add 2 tablespoons of this to the pan, stirring well. After a few minutes, add another 2 tablespoons, again stirring. Finally add the rest of this mixture. Cover the pan and cook gently until the chicken is tender, 45 to 60 minutes depending on the tenderness of the chicken.

Take out the chicken pieces and place on a warm serving dish. Stir the sauce well, add the remaining cream and wine and bring gently to the boil. Pour a little over the chicken pieces and serve the rest separately.

Serve with sautéed potatoes and with stewed fruit such as prunes, pears, apples or cherries, or a green salad.

## STUFFED CAPON (*Töltött csirke*)   Hungary

6–8 servings:
5lb (2¼kg) capon
salt, freshly ground pepper to taste
1 bread roll
1 cup milk
¼lb (125g) calf's liver
2 slices bacon, diced

fresh or dried marjoram to taste
2 eggs, well beaten
½lb (250g) mushrooms, cleaned and chopped
1tb parsley, finely chopped
4oz (125g,½cup) butter or goose fat
½pt (¼l,1¼cups) red wine
¼pt (1dl,⅔cup) sour cream

Rub the capon with salt and leave for 1 hour. Soak the bread in milk and squeeze dry. Wash the liver thoroughly in warm water. Remove the skin and cut out any bits of fat and tissue. Drain, dry and cut into pieces. Trim the capon liver and gizzard and put through the fine blade of a mincer with the calf's liver and the bread roll. Put this mixture into a bowl. Add the bacon, salt, pepper, marjoram and eggs and knead the mixture thoroughly. Chill for 30 minutes. Combine the mushrooms and parsley. Lift up the skin of the capon carefully (it can be done with the handle of a wooden spoon) and loosen it from the breast. Push the liver stuffing under the skin and ease it down to spread evenly all over the breast. Smooth the skin back into place. Stuff the mushroom and parsley mixture into the cavity of the capon. Place the capon on the rack of a roasting pan. Heat the butter or goose fat and pour it over the bird. Add half the wine.

Roast in a moderate oven (350°F: 180°C: Gas 4) until tender, allowing 25 minutes to the pound, basting frequently and each time adding a little more of the wine but retaining some for the gravy. If the capon is browning too quickly, cover it with foil. When tender, take the capon from the pan, put aside and keep hot. Add the sour cream and the remaining wine to the gravy in the pan. Stir well, scraping the sides and bottom of the pan to collect the sediment. Reheat the sauce on top of the stove, strain and serve in a sauceboat.

Serve the capon with sauté or roast potatoes and vegetables in season.

## ROAST DUCK (*Töltött kacsa*)   Hungary

3–4 servings:
1 duck, 4–5lb (2–2½kg, 4–5lb)
salt to taste
4 anchovy fillets, mashed
2oz (60g, ¼cup) butter or other fat
½ lemon rind, grated
1tb capers
4tb (5tb) soft breadcrumbs
2 eggs, beaten
¼pt (1dl, ⅔cup) stock
¼pt (1dl, ⅔cup) red wine

Rub the outside of the duck with salt. Mix the anchovy fillets, butter, lemon rind, capers and breadcrumbs with the beaten eggs. Push this mixture inside the duck. Place the duck breast side down in a deep casserole, add the stock and wine, cover and bake in a moderate oven (350°F: 180°C: Gas 4) for 1 hour, then turn the bird over and bake uncovered for another 30 minutes. If the duck appears to be browning too quickly, cover with foil. Take the duck from the casserole, remove the trussing strings, carve and arrange it on a hot dish. Keep hot. Drain off and strain the liquid in the casserole and use as gravy.

The Hungarians take the duck liver, slice it thinly and use it as a garnish. Roast potatoes and sliced green beans are recommended as accompaniments.

## DUCK WITH SAUERKRAUT (*Ente mit Sauerkraut*)   South Germany

3 servings:
4lb (2kg) duck
3oz (90g, 6tb) fat
salt to taste
1½lb (¾kg) sauerkraut
¼pt (1dl, ⅔cup) red wine
¼pt (1dl, ⅔cup) sour cream

Cut the duck into portions and carefully remove the breast bone, keeping the pieces of meat as large as possible. Rub the portions with a little fat, sprinkle lightly with salt and leave for 1 hour. Heat the remaining fat in a pan and quickly fry the duck pieces to a golden brown. Put a layer of sauerkraut on the bottom of an ovenproof casserole, arrange the duck pieces on top, add the duck liver, thinly sliced, and cover with the rest of the sauerkraut. Mix the wine and the sour cream together and spoon this mixture over the top. Cover and cook in a moderate oven (350°F: 180°C: Gas 4) for 1 to 1½ hours. Do not overcook or the sauerkraut will become a rather sad brown. Serve in the casserole with dumplings (see page 136) or potatoes.

### ROAST GOOSE (*Pečeně husa*)  Czechoslovakia

4–6 servings:
6lb (2½kg) goose
salt to taste
1tsp caraway seeds

Rub the goose all over with salt. Place in a baking pan on its breast and sprinkle with caraway seeds. Add about 1 cupful of boiling water to the pan. This helps the skin to steam and release the goose fat, very important if the goose is very fat. Roast in a moderate oven (350°F: 180°C: Gas 4) basting frequently and from time to time prick the surface of the skin to help the fat flow. After the goose has been cooking for about 30 minutes, turn it over. Continue roasting until the flesh is tender and the skin a good golden colour. Take from the oven and cut into portions.

A young goose will take approximately 1 to 1½ hours to cook; older ones take 2 hours or more.

Duck also is cooked in the same manner. In Czechoslovakia it is usual to serve small dumplings (see page 130) and sauerkraut with goose (or duck); both counteract the richness of the meat.

## ROAST STUFFED GOOSE (*Sült liba*)  Hungary

8–10 servings:
10–12lb (4½kg) plump goose
salt, pepper to taste
4 eggs, hard-boiled and coarsely chopped
1lb (½kg) mushrooms, coarsely chopped
¼pt (1dl,⅔cup) sour cream
1tsp finely chopped chives
pinch marjoram
2 eggs, beaten
2tb (2½tb) red wine
2oz (60g,¼cup) goose or pork fat
1tb flour

Rub the goose all over with salt and leave for 2 hours. In the meantime prepare the stuffing. Put into a deep bowl the hard-boiled eggs, mushrooms, sour cream, chives, the goose liver cut into small pieces, salt, pepper, a good pinch of marjoram, beaten eggs and wine. Mix well and stuff the mixture into the cavity of the goose; pin the skin flaps together with small skewers. Spread the fat on a piece of foil, cover the goose with this and put it on to the rack of a baking pan. Add just enough water to cover the bottom of the pan. Roast in a hot oven (425°F: 220°C: Gas 7) for 30 minutes. Reduce the heat and continue roasting until the goose is tender, basting frequently. After the first hour, discard the foil and let the goose brown.

To make the gravy, drain off all but 2 tablespoons of the fat in the pan, add the flour to the pan, mix together and add enough clear stock or water to make a thin gravy. Cook for 5 minutes.

Roast goose is rich so serve it simply with a green salad, letting the gravy and the stuffing be sufficient garnish. However, red cabbage or any of the early greens are served with goose in Hungary.

The usual cooking time for a 10 to 12lb goose is between 2 and 2½ hours.

## STEAMED PHEASANT (*Pàrolt Fàcàn*)   Hungary

3–4 servings:
1 pheasant
2oz (60g,4tb) butter or other fat
½ small onion, peeled and sliced
2 carrots, sliced
salt, peppercorns to taste
2 strips lemon rind
½pt (¼l,1¼cups) red wine
¼pt (1dl,⅔cup) fresh or sour cream

Heat the butter in a casserole and lightly fry the onion and carrots until they begin to change colour. Add the pheasant, salt, peppercorns, lemon rind and the red wine. Cover and cook over a low heat until the pheasant is tender. Check from time to time to see the liquid has not evaporated. If it has, add a little more. When the pheasant is cooked, take it from the pan, put aside but keep hot. Rub the gravy through a fine sieve, combine with the cream, return to the casserole and gently bring to the boil. The average pheasant will take from 40 to 45 minutes to cook.

Carve the pheasant into serving pieces, pour the sauce over the top and serve with potato crisps or Saratoga chips.

## STEWED PIGEONS (*Gedünstete Tauben*)   Austria

3–6 servings:
3 pigeons or squabs
½lb (¼kg) mushrooms
1 mild onion
¼lb (125g) lean ham
3oz (90g,6tb) butter
salt, pepper to taste
1 bay leaf
2–3 thin strips lemon peel
½pt (¼l,1¼cups) dry white wine
½pt (¼l,1¼cups) water, warm

Wash and thinly slice the mushrooms. Mince the onion and dice the ham. Heat the butter in a flameproof casserole. Add the pigeons and gently but lightly brown them all over. Take from the pan, put aside but keep warm.

In the same fat cook the onion and mushrooms for 2 to 3 minutes. Return the pigeons and sprinkle with salt and pepper. Add the ham, bay leaf and lemon peel, then the wine and water. Bring gently to the boil then cover tightly with foil or a lid or both. Transfer the casserole to a low oven (300°F: 150°C: Gas 1–2) and continue cooking for about 1 hour but check after about 45 minutes. Cooking time depends on the age of the birds. Remove the bay leaf and lemon peel before serving.

Serve with rice, puréed potatoes and a green salad.

## QUAIL, TRANSYLVANIAN STYLE (*Fürj Székely Mòdra*)   Hungary

3 servings:
3 quail, halved
¼lb (125g) sliced fat bacon
1lb (½kg) sauerkraut
1 medium-sized smoked sausage, sliced
3–4 sour apples
salt, pepper to taste
½pt (¼l, 1¼cups) white wine

Line an ovenproof casserole with bacon, spread over this a layer of sauerkraut, another layer of bacon then a layer of sausage. Peel and slice the apples and spread half of them in a layer over the top of the sausages. Place the quail halves on top. Sprinkle each layer with salt and pepper. Repeat layers of bacon, sausage and apple, finishing with the rest of the sauerkraut. Pour the wine over the top and bake in a moderately hot oven (350°F: 180°C: Gas 4) uncovered for 30 to 45 minutes, basting frequently with the sauce in the casserole.

The type of smoked sausage used in this recipe is *kolbàsz* but any well-flavoured smoked sausage can be used instead. Whether one or two sausages are required depends on the size of the sausage chosen, two layers are required.

In Britain there is a clear distinction between the hare and the rabbit, whereas in the United States this does not appear to be the case. In the south the hare is called Old Hare regardless of its age. In the north hares are popularly called The Snowshoe Rabbit, Jack Rabbit, and there is also a Prairie Rabbit.

## HARE HUNTER'S STYLE (*Hasenjunges Jägerart*)   South Germany

6–7 servings:
1 young hare
black pepper, freshly ground to taste
ground ginger to taste
1tb wine vinegar
dry red wine to cover
6 cloves
12 juniper berries, crushed
6 thin slices fat bacon
2oz (60g,4tb) lard

Only the saddle and the back of the hare are used for roasting.

Rub the hare generously with pepper and ground ginger, then put into an earthenware casserole, add the vinegar and cover with red wine. Add the cloves and juniper berries. Leave overnight in a cool place.

Next day take the hare from the marinade. Drain and wipe dry. Cover the back with the bacon. Place on the rack of a roasting pan. Heat the lard to boiling and pour this over the hare. Put the pan into a hot oven (425°F: 220°C: Gas 7) and roast the hare at this heat for 15 minutes. Reduce the heat to moderate (350°F: 180°C: Gas 4), add a cupful of the marinade and continue roasting, basting with the rest of the marinade until the hare is tender.

Take the hare from the pan and put on to a hot dish. Skim off the surplus fat from the pan, scrape round the sides of the pan and bring the gravy to the boil. Pour through a sieve and serve in a sauceboat.

Serve the hare with puréed potatoes, red cabbage and redcurrant sauce.

If using only the saddle of the hare, it will serve only 3 to 4; if using the saddle and hindquarters, 5 to 6. Cooking time is about 1½ hours.

## HARE RAGOÛT (*Hasenragout*)  South Germany

4–6 servings:
2–2½lb (1–1¼kg) hare
green herbs to taste
1 each carrot, celery stalk, small parsnip
1 bay leaf
salt, pepper to taste
4 slices fat bacon, diced
1 small onion, finely chopped
1tb sugar
¼–½pt (1–2dl,⅔–1¼cups) red wine
1tb lemon juice

The hare should be cut into pieces. Put it into a pan adding boiling water to well cover. Add the herbs, vegetables, bay leaf, salt and pepper and cook over a moderate heat until the meat is almost but not quite tender.

In another pan fry the bacon until the fat runs, add the onion and fry until it is a golden brown. Add the sugar, let this brown, then add the wine and the lemon juice and stir well. Pour this sauce over the hare and continue cooking until it is quite tender.

Take the hare pieces from the pan and place on a hot plate. Rub the sauce through a sieve, pour this over the hare and serve with puréed potatoes, or bread or potato dumplings (see pages 131, 135).

## RABBIT WITH BLACK SAUCE (*Zajíc na Černe*)  Czechoslovakia

4–6 servings:

1 rabbit
3 slices fat bacon, diced
½oz (15g,1tb) butter or other fat
1 large onion, peeled and
finely chopped
1 bay leaf
¼tsp thyme

5 peppercorns
salt to taste
2–3 strips lemon rind
1oz (30g,2tb) butter or other fat
½oz (15g,2tb) flour
1tb brown sugar
juice of 1 lemon

Cut the rabbit into serving pieces and wipe with a damp cloth. Fry the bacon in a large pan until the fat begins to run. Add the first quantity of butter and, when this has melted, add the onion and cook gently until it begins to change colour. Add the herbs, peppercorns and salt, then the pieces of rabbit, the lemon rind and enough water to cover. Cover and cook gently until the rabbit is tender.

In another pan heat the second quantity of butter, add the flour and stir to a brown roux. Gradually add enough of the liquid from the simmering rabbit to make a thick gravy. Add the sugar, lemon juice (or the equivalent in mild vinegar) and cook for 5 to 6 minutes.

Take the rabbit pieces from the pan, place on a hot dish but keep warm. Stir the gravy through a fine sieve over the rabbit.

Serve with dumplings or boiled or mashed potatoes.


### ROAST VENISON (*Srnčí Pečeně*)  Czechoslovakia

4–6 servings:
2–2½lb (1kg) venison
2oz (60g,4tb) fat bacon, cut into strips
3oz (90g,6tb) fat
1 onion, peeled and chopped
salt, pepper to taste
6 juniper berries    1tsp flour

Wipe the meat with a damp cloth and thread strips of bacon or larding through the flesh across the 'grain' with a larding needle or skewer. Heat the fat in a large baking pan. Add the meat and fry until brown all over. Add the onion, salt and pepper, juniper berries and enough hot water to prevent burning. Bake in a moderate oven (350°F: 180°C: Gas 4) until tender. Baste frequently with hot water. When the meat is tender, take it from the pan, place on a warm dish, put aside but keep hot. Sprinkle the flour into the gravy, stir it well and cook for 5 minutes. Strain and serve poured over the meat with boiled potatoes, rice, noodles or dumplings.

Note: venison takes a long time to cook, at least 2 to 2½ hours, and it must be basted again and again otherwise the meat will be dry. The best joint for roasting is the haunch but the fillet, loin and neck may be used.

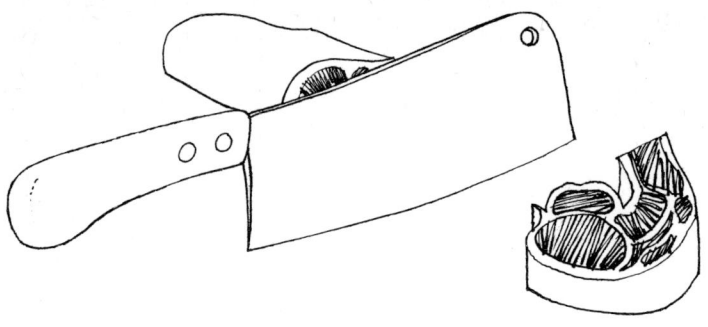

# MEAT

### MARINATED BEEF (*Sauerbraten*)   South Germany

This is served as a special dish for weddings, birthdays or maybe a family gathering. The recipe varies according to the district.

10–12 servings:
4–5lb (2–2½kg) beef, for pot roasting
½lb (¼kg) very lean bacon
2oz (60g,4tb) dripping or other fat
3 thick slices black bread or ginger cake, crumbled

for marinade:

½pt (¼l,1¼cups) white wine or vinegar
1pt (½l,2½cups) red wine
2 medium-sized onions, peeled and sliced
6 peppercorns
6 juniper berries, crushed
2–3 cloves
1 bay leaf
2tsp salt

Cut the bacon into thin strips and lard the meat or push the pieces of bacon through the meat with a skewer. Combine the marinade ingredients. Place the meat in a large bowl or, better still, an earthenware pot and add the marinade. If the meat is not quite covered, add more marinade. Leave in a cool place, in summer for about 3 days, in winter 5. Take the meat from the pot and let it drain through a sieve.

Heat the fat in a large pan, add the drained meat and fry until brown all over. Add the marinade, cover the pan and cook over a simmering heat for 3 hours, or until the meat is tender. The meat must not be allowed to cook quickly.

When the meat is tender, take it from the pan, place on a hot plate and keep warm. Rub the sauce through a fine sieve, mix with the crumbled black bread or ginger cake and cook in a smaller pan until the sauce is thick and dark—but do not let it boil.

Serve the meat cut into good thick slices in a fairly deep plate and pour over the sauce. *Spätzle*, dumplings or noodles are served with *Sauerbraten* in the South, and a green salad. Topside or round of buttocks is the best cut to use for this dish.

## SLICED BOILED BEEF (*Tellerfleisch*)   South Germany

This is a family recipe and does not have exact quantities. *Tellerfleisch* consists of good quality beef cooked in a stock or in well-flavoured water, that is, with salt, pepper, herbs and root vegetables, until tender. It is then cut into thin slices and served on a wooden platter. A little of the hot stock is poured over the top and the meat is then sprinkled lightly with finely chopped chives and grated horseradish.

*Tellerfleisch* can be served at luncheon but more often it is served at *gabelfrühstück* or second breakfast.

## BOILED BEEF (*Tafelspitz*)   Austria

As with all such dishes, it is cheapest in the long run to buy a large cut of meat. This must be neatly tied so that it will not come apart in the cooking, and be easier to slice. Serve either hot or cold.

10–12 servings:
4lb (2kg) beef
2 carrots
2 celery stalks
1 large onion, peeled
2 tomatoes
1 small parsnip
salt to taste
chives, finely chopped, to garnish

Prepare the vegetables. Cut the carrots into lengths, the celery into 2 or 3 pieces, the onion in quarters, the tomatoes into halves, and the parsnip into thick rounds. Put all these into a large pan, add the meat, salt and plenty of cold water. Bring gently to the boil, lower the heat and let the water simmer so that it hardly moves for 4 to 5 hours. Do not remove the scum and keep the pan covered all the time.

To serve, take the meat from the pan and cut into medium-thick slices, sprinkle with chives and serve with *apfelkren* (see page 125) and fried or sautéed potatoes.

Strain the stock and use it as a clear soup or bouillon.


BEEF STEW (*Marhatokàny*)   Hungary

A *Tokàny* is a stew and there are many kinds, varying from district to district. Choose shin of beef, stewing steak, chuck or shank.

4–6 servings:
2lb (1kg) beef
½lb (250g) onions
3oz (90g,6tb) lard or shortening
½pt (¼l,1¼cups) tomato juice
1tb paprika pepper
salt, caraway seeds to taste
garlic to taste
pinch marjoram to taste

Wash and dry the meat and trim off skin and fat. Cut the meat into stew-size pieces and peel and slice the onions coarsely. Heat the lard in a large pan. Add the onions and cook slowly stirring frequently, until they begin to change colour. Add the meat and cook for 5 minutes, turning it from time to time. Add the remaining ingredients. Cook gently without adding any more liquid unless the liquid has reduced too much during cooking; check from time to time to see the meat is not drying out. If all the liquid has evaporated, add a little warm water. Keep the pan covered and cook for 1½ to 2 hours or until the meat is tender.

Serve the meat with its sauce and boiled potatoes.

## BEEF STEW (*Rindsgulasch*)   Austria

The Austrians, in particular the Viennese, are careful to explain that while *gulyàs* is a Hungarian dish, *Gulasch* is Austrian. It resembles more the Hungarian *pörkölt* and is usually prepared with beef, veal, chicken and pork, but there is even a sausage and liver version.

4–6 servings:
2lb (1kg) rump steak, cubed
4oz (125g,½cup) fat
2lb (1kg) onions, peeled and sliced     1tb paprika pepper
1pt (½l,2½cups) hot stock, or water     1tsp salt

The 'secret' of this particular recipe is the equal quantity of meat to onions.

Heat the fat, add the onions and cook gently until they begin to change colour. Add the paprika and stir thoroughly. Add the meat (the cubes should be the usual stew-size) raise the heat and cook the meat until brown. Gradually add enough liquid to just cover the meat, lower the heat, add the salt, cover the pan and continue cooking until the meat is tender; the time will depend on the quality of the meat. Add the rest of the stock.

To the above may be added: 1 crushed clove of garlic with the onions and, after adding the stock, 1 teaspoon caraway seeds, a bay leaf or a bouquet garni, ½ teaspoon of ground ginger, sage or parsley, and cloves.

Instead of stock or water, a mixture of both can be used, or stock flavoured with red or even white wine.

## HUNTER'S BEEF (*Jägerbraten*) Austria

4–6 servings:
2lb (1kg) beef
3–4 thin slices fat bacon, cut into strips
3oz (90g,6tb) butter or other fat
1 each carrot, parsnip, small head celery,
leek, cleaned and sliced
1 large onion, sliced
1 bay leaf
thyme to taste
5 peppercorns
salt to taste
2–3 strips lemon peel
$\frac{1}{4}$pt (1dl,$\frac{2}{3}$cup) red wine
1tb sugar
1 small onion, peeled and finely chopped
1 small gherkin, chopped
parsley, finely chopped, to taste
5 capers
1tb flour

Beat the meat until it is flat and thread with the thin strips of bacon, using a larding needle or skewer. Rub a large pan with half the butter, add the meat, cover with the vegetables, herbs, peppercorns, salt, lemon peel and wine—a little more wine or water may be required during cooking. Cover and cook the meat over a moderate heat until tender.

Take the meat from the pan, put aside but keep hot. Rub the gravy through a sieve. In the same pan heat the remaining butter, add the sugar, the finely chopped onion, gherkin, parsley and capers, and lightly cook for 5 minutes. Add the flour, stir it well, add the sieved gravy, mix well, cook for 5 minutes, then return the meat to the pan and simmer it for about 15 minutes.

Serve the meat in its sauce with mashed potatoes.

## BEEF OLIVES (*Gombàshus*)   Hungary

6 servings:
1lb (½kg) thick rump steak
4oz (125g,½cup) fat
½lb (250g) mushrooms, coarsely chopped
1 small red onion, peeled and finely chopped
salt, pepper to taste

Heat half the fat in a fairly large pan. Add the mushrooms and onion and fry until the mushrooms are soft. Take both the mushrooms and onion from the pan with a perforated spoon. Put aside but keep hot.

Cut the steak into 6 slices about ¼ inch thick. Pound firmly, but not too heavily, with a cutlet bat until very thin but do not break the meat. In the middle of each piece of meat put a portion of the mushroom and onion mixture, sprinkle with salt and pepper, roll up tightly and tie with thread. Heat the rest of the fat in the same pan, add the beef rolls (olives) and brown them lightly all over. Add water to just cover, cover the pan and stew gently for 1½ hours, basting frequently. As the liquid cooks away or evaporates, add more warm water. Can be served with mashed potatoes, rice, noodles or fried potato cakes.

## BEEF ROLLS OR OLIVES (*Rindsroulade*)   Austria

6 servings:
6 thick slices steak
salt, pepper to taste
¼lb (125g) belly of pork, chopped
1–2 pickled gherkins, sliced lengthwise
1 medium-sized onion, coarsely chopped
parsley, finely chopped, to taste
3 anchovy fillets, chopped
6 capers, chopped      flour
2oz (60g,6tb) pork fat
1 small onion, finely chopped
½pt (¼l,1¼cups) sour cream      stock to dilute

Beat the steaks until very thin but the meat is not broken. Sprinkle lightly with salt and pepper. On each slice put a little belly of pork, gherkin, onion, parsley, anchovy and 1 caper. Roll up each slice of meat tightly, making sure none of the ingredients can fall out of the sides. Tie securely with thread and roll lightly in flour. Heat the pork fat in a pan and gently add the beef rolls. Fry the rolls until brown all over, then take from the pan. Fry the finely chopped onion until it changes colour, sprinkle in 1 tablespoon of flour and stir for a few minutes. Gradually add the sour cream, stirring all the time, and dilute with just enough stock or water to make a medium-thick gravy. Return the rolls to the pan and continue cooking for another 30 minutes, or until the meat is tender.

To serve the rolls, take them from the pan, remove the threads and place rolls on a dish. Rub the gravy through a sieve and quickly pour over the rolls. Serve with mashed potatoes, rice and noodles.

## BRAISED GIPSY ROAST (*Cikánská Pečeně*)   Czechoslovakia

4–6 servings:
1½–2lb (¾–1kg) beef, chuck steak

For stuffing:

2–3 slices bacon, diced
3 eggs
2oz (60g,4tb) dripping, just melted
1 bread roll
3tb (4tb) milk
½lb (250g) ground pork or sausage meat
½ small onion, finely chopped
2oz (60g,1cup) ham, finely chopped (optional)
salt, pepper to taste
dried marjoram, ground ginger and ground allspice to taste
1tb flour

For braising:

1oz (30g,2tb) fat
1 medium-sized onion, finely sliced
root vegetables, sliced (see method)
½lb (250g) mushrooms

Pound the meat with a cutlet bat until very thin but still in one whole piece. Fry the bacon until crisp and take from pan. Fry the eggs in the bacon fat; when the whites have just begun to set, break the yolks gently with a fork so that they spread evenly over the egg whites. It helps when spreading the fried eggs over the stuffing.

Place the pounded meat on a board. Rub it with the melted dripping. Soak the bread roll in the milk and squeeze until dry. Spread the pork or sausage meat over the meat, add the bread roll, spreading it almost to the edge of the meat and pressing down well. Instead of using ground pork or sausage meat, extra bread may be used. Over this place the fried eggs, sprinkle with the bacon and chopped onion. If using ham, add this now. Sprinkle with salt, pepper, marjoram, ginger and allspice. Carefully roll up the meat tightly and tie securely with string. Sprinkle lightly with flour.

Heat the braising fat in a casserole, add the sliced onion and root vegetables. These are seasonal, ie a turnip, carrot, stalk of celery, or a small parsnip. Fry these ingredients until they change colour. Add the meat roll and just enough warm water to well cover the bottom of the casserole to prevent sticking. Cover and cook gently until the meat is tender, the time depends on the quality of the meat but one can reckon up to $1\frac{1}{2}$ to 2 hours.

Wash and slice the mushrooms, caps and stems, add these to the pan about 30 minutes before the meat is ready.

To serve, take the meat from the pan, remove the strings and slice the meat thickly. Place the slices on a hot dish. Use the mushrooms and root vegetables as a garnish. Pour the sauce through a sieve over the meat.

Serve hot or cold with rice, dumplings, or mashed potatoes.

## HUSSAR'S BEEF (*Husarská Svíčková*)   Czechoslovakia

4–6 servings:
2lb (1kg) beef (see method)
2tsp paprika pepper
lemon juice to taste
5–6 slices fat bacon
1oz (30g, 2tb) butter or other fat
1 medium-sized onion, peeled and chopped
pinch of thyme
1 bay leaf
salt to taste
6 peppercorns
6 allspice (whole, not ground)
2tb (2½tb) vinegar
1tsp grated lemon rind
½pt (¼l, 1¼cups) sour cream
1tb flour

The original recipe called for fillet steak or tenderloin. However, sirloin or ribs on the bone, boned and rolled, can be used instead.

Trim the meat, removing any skin, membranes etc and flatten with a cutlet bat. Sprinkle with paprika pepper and lemon juice and cover with the bacon slices. Roll it lightly and tie with string. Heat the butter, add the onion and fry for a few minutes. Add the meat and brown it all round. Add the herbs, salt, peppercorns, allspice, vinegar, lemon rind and enough water to prevent burning. Place in a baking pan and bake in a moderate oven (350°F: 180°C: Gas 4) until tender, basting from time to time.

When meat is almost tender, add half the sour cream. Continue basting from time to time until the meat is very tender and turn it occasionally. Cooking time depends on the quality of the meat but cook certainly up to 2 hours. Take the meat from the pan, put aside but keep hot. Transfer the baking pan to the top of the stove, mix the flour with a little more cream and stir into the gravy. Bring to the boil, stir in the rest of the cream and continue cooking, stirring all the time, until the sauce is thick.

Take the strings from the meat, cut the meat into slices and strain the sauce over it. Serve with dumplings, boiled potatoes or noodles.

## ESZTERHAZY STEAK (*Eszterhàzy rostèlyos*)  Hungary

Eszterhàzy is the name of a family prominent in Hungary since the thirteenth century. At one time the largest landowners in Hungary, they were great supporters of the Habsburgs, and a large number of dishes have been named after them.

6 servings:
2lb (1kg) rump steak, 1 inch thick
flour    salt, pepper to taste
2oz (60g,4tb) fat
3 carrots, thinly sliced
2 small onions, thinly sliced
1 parsnip, thinly sliced
1 celery stalk, chopped
1–3tsp capers
½pt (¼l,1¼cups) clear meat stock, lukewarm
¼pt (1dl,⅔cup) dry white wine
½pt (¼l,1¼cups) fresh, or sour, thick cream
2tsp paprika pepper

Wipe the meat with a damp cloth, sprinkle it with flour and pound with a cutlet bat. Turn the meat and repeat the process. Cut the meat into 6 steaks. Dip in flour and sprinkle lightly with salt and pepper. Heat half the fat in a heavy frying pan, add the steaks and brown well on both sides. Take from the pan and place in a greased baking dish. Add the prepared vegetables to the frying pan, stir and cook for 10 minutes. Spread the vegetables over the meat and add the capers.

Heat the remaining fat in the frying pan, add 1 tablespoon flour and salt and pepper to taste. Stir until the mixture is smooth and begins to bubble. Gradually add the stock and the wine and stir to a thick gravy. Stir for a few minutes, then pour the gravy over the steaks. Cover the baking dish with foil and bake in a moderate oven (350°F: 180°C: Gas 4) for about 1¼ hours or until the meat is tender. Remove the foil, add the cream, sprinkle with paprika and bake for a further 15 minutes.

The meat can be cooked on top of the stove. It should be cooked until it is so tender it can easily be pierced with a fork.

### FRIED STEAKS WITH ONIONS (*Zwiebelrostbraten*)   Austria

Also called *Wiener Rostbraten*, this recipe calls for good quality steaks.

4 servings:
4 tender steaks
salt, pepper to taste
flour, for coating
2 large onions
3oz (90g,6tb) pork dripping
½ cup clear stock, hot

Trim all fat off steaks, beat them well but without breaking the meat, and nick them slightly round the edges. Sprinkle lightly with salt and pepper, and coat with flour on one side only. Peel and slice the onions into thin rounds.

Heat fat until it is very hot, add onions and cook until rich brown. Take from the pan, put aside but keep hot. Add the steaks, floured side underneath, and fry them quickly. When brown on one side, turn and brown the other side. The steaks should be cooked somewhat rare. Pour the stock over the top of the steaks and serve at once, garnished with the fried onions. Serve with fried potatoes and sliced gherkins.

### SWABIAN STEAKS (*Schwäbischer Rostbraten*)   South Germany

4–6 servings:
4–6 beef fillets
pinch of pepper
flour, for coating
fat for frying
½lb (¼kg) onions, peeled and thickly sliced
¼pt (1dl,⅔cup) sour cream

The fillets should all be of the same size. Beat them, not too much, sprinkle with pepper and coat with flour. Heat a little fat in a large pan and quickly fry the meat on both sides until brown. Then add more fat, enough in which to continue cooking the meat without it burning. Add the onions, let these cook until they begin to change colour, cover the pan and continue cooking over a low heat until the meat is tender.

To serve, take the meat from the pan, place on a hot dish, add the onions and spread these over the meat. Keep it warm while you make a sauce. Add the sour cream to the fat in the pan and cook for a few minutes, stirring all the time. Pour it over the meat.

This dish is served with *Spätzle* (see page 143) and with all kinds of green salads as well as tomato and radish salads.


## TRANSYLVANIAN MEAT PIE (*Erdèlyi hùs*)   Hungary

4–6 servings:
1lb (½kg) stewing steak
2½oz (75g,5tb) fat
1 bunch parsley, finely chopped
salt, pepper, French mustard to taste
2 bread rolls
milk, water or wine, for soaking
1tb tomato paste
1pt (½l,2½cups) fresh, or sour, cream
1oz (30g,2tb) butter
grated cheese to garnish

Dice the meat. Heat the fat in a small pan, add the meat, parsley and a little salt. Cook the meat until tender. Soak the bread rolls in the milk, water or wine until soft and squeeze dry. Put these, together with the cooked meat, through the coarse blade of a grinder. Flavour to taste with salt, pepper and French mustard. Add the tomato paste and the cream, and mix well. Rub a baking dish with some of the butter. Add the meat mixture and shape it into a cone. Melt the remaining butter and pour this over the top of the cone and bake in a moderate oven (350°F: 180°C: Gas 4) for about 30 minutes. Just before serving, sprinkle with grated cheese.

This dish is a little rich but it makes a pound of meat go a long way. It can be served with potatoes, rice, pasta and preferably also with green vegetables, such as peas or green beans.

## ESCALOPES

The average weight of an escalope is from 4 to 5oz. It is a thin slice or fillet of veal which is cut from the fillet, best end of neck, or topside. For a *Schnitzel*, it is beaten until it is very thin indeed, sometimes—it must be confessed—until the meat loses its flavour. I have seen *Schnitzels* in Vienna about the same size as the plates on which they were served.

### PLAIN ESCALOPES (*Schnitzel Natur*)   Austria

4 servings:
4 veal escalopes
salt to taste
flour, for dredging
fat, for frying
1tb stock or water
knob of butter
lemon wedges, for serving

Do not wash the escalopes but wipe them with a damp cloth, make a few incisions round the edge of each piece of meat and beat thoroughly. Sprinkle lightly with salt and dredge one side of each escalope lightly with flour. Heat enough fat to cover the bottom of the frying pan. When very hot, add 2 (no more) of the escalopes and fry the unfloured side first as quickly and as evenly as possible until brown. Turn, and fry the other side. Place the escalopes on a warm plate and repeat with the remaining escalopes. Pour off surplus fat but keep the little brown bits of juice from the meat in the pan. Add the stock or water and butter and stir well to make a gravy. Pour this over the meat and serve at once with wedges of lemon.

The reason for frying so few escalopes at one time is that the liquid which flows from them causes them to simmer rather than fry. They must be served immediately after cooking otherwise they will become tough.

## ESCALOPES HOLSTEIN (*Holstein Schnitzel*)   Austria

Escalopes Holstein are cooked in the same way as Plain Escalopes but a fried egg is placed on each and they are garnished with anchovy fillets and capers, and served with lemon wedges.

## ESCALOPES PARIS (*Pariser Schnitzel*)   Austria

Prepare 4 escalopes as for Plain Escalopes. Heat the fat. Sprinkle each escalope lightly with salt and dip each into well-beaten egg and fry immediately in the hot fat until a golden brown on both sides. Serve at once.

## EMPEROR ESCALOPES (*Kaiser Schnitzel*)   Austria

For this recipe the escalopes are a little smaller but cooked in the same way as for Plain Escalopes. When they are brown, lift them from the pan and place on a hot dish. Add a few tablespoons of cream to the pan, stir and when the sauce has become thick and yellowish, add 1 to 3 tablespoons of lemon juice and some finely chopped lemon rind. Pour this sauce over the meat and serve immediately.

## WIENER SCHNITZEL (*Wiener Schnitzel*)   Austria

4 servings:
4 veal escalopes
salt to taste
flour, for dredging
1 large egg, well beaten
fine breadcrumbs, for coating
cooking fat, for deep frying
lemon wedges, for serving

Trim the escalopes as for Plain Escalopes. Beat them until quite flat. Have ready three shallow bowls or soup plates. In one put flour, in another the beaten egg, and in the third the breadcrumbs. Heat the fat in a frying pan. Dip the escalopes first in the flour, shake off surplus, then in the beaten egg and finally in the breadcrumbs. Do not press the coating down but let the escalopes rest for about 10 minutes. Fry each escalope in very hot fat first on one side until brown, then the other. Drain the escalopes on kitchen paper and serve with wedges of lemon and sautéed potatoes and a green salad.

It is not possible to give the exact quantity of either flour or fine bread-crumbs for coating. Different cooks coat thinly or thickly as their taste dictates.

### VEAL STEW WITH DUMPLINGS (*Zedělávané telecí s knedlíčky*)
Czechoslovakia

4–6 servings:
2lb (1kg) boneless veal, breast or shoulder
1 carrot
1 small piece celeriac or celery stalk
1 small piece parsley root or parsnip
1½oz (45g,3tb) butter or other fat
2tb flour
2 strips lemon rind
1tb lemon juice
¼tsp ground mace or nutmeg
parsley, coarsely chopped, to taste
salt to taste
bread dumplings (see page 131)

Blanch the veal by bringing to the boil in cold water, and boiling for 15 minutes. Take from the pan, drain, cool and cut into stew-size pieces. Clean the vegetables and cut into small pieces. Heat the butter, add the vegetables and fry until they begin to change colour. Dredge with flour and stir it well into the vegetables, then add enough warm water to make a thick sauce, stirring all the time. Cook for 5 minutes fairly rapidly, then add lemon rind and juice, mace, parsley and salt. Stir well, add the meat, lower the heat and simmer until the meat is tender. If required, add a little more warm water but the stew should not be too liquid. The cooking time will depend on the quality of the meat—$1\frac{1}{2}$ hours should be enough.

Prepare the bread dumplings (see page 131). About 15 minutes before the meat is ready, drop the dumplings into a pan of boiling, lightly salted water. When they rise to the top of the liquid they are ready. Take from the pan with a perforated spoon and add to the stew 5 minutes before serving.

Serve with fried mushrooms and boiled cauliflower.


## LAMB CHOPS WITH DILL SAUCE (*Bàrànykottlet Kapormàrtàssal*)
Hungary

6 servings:
6 $\frac{1}{2}$-inch thick lamb chops
$1\frac{1}{2}$oz (45g,3tb) fat
1 medium-sized onion, peeled and finely chopped
2tb water
1tb mild or wine vinegar
salt, pepper to taste
1 bay leaf

For sauce:

1oz (30g,2tb) butter or other fat
$\frac{1}{2}$oz (15g,2tb) flour
salt, pepper to taste
$\frac{1}{2}$pt ($\frac{1}{4}$l,1$\frac{1}{4}$cups) water or stock
1tb fresh dill or fennel, finely chopped
$\frac{1}{4}$pt (1dl,$\frac{2}{3}$cup) dry white wine

Heat the fat in a fairly large, heavy frying pan, add the onion and slowly cook until it begins to change colour. Take this from the pan with a perforated spoon and put aside. Wipe the chops with a cloth, trim off surplus fat or skin and cut through the fat on the outside edges at intervals of about 1 inch. Take care not to cut through into the lean meat. Put all the chops into the pan at the same time and fry slowly on one side until brown, then turn and brown the other side.

While the meat is cooking, combine the next 4 ingredients. Pour this mixture over the chops, then return the onion, spreading it evenly. Cover pan and continue cooking until the meat is tender. Test with a fork and, if needed, add a little more water to the pan from time to time.

To make the sauce, heat the butter in a small pan, add the flour and stir it to make a roux. Add salt and pepper and, stirring continuously, cook until the roux is a golden brown. Gradually add the liquid, stirring all the time, until the sauce is thick. Take the pan from the stove, add the dill, then return the pan to the stove and rapidly boil the sauce for 1 minute. Take from the stove, gradually add the wine, stirring all the time. Pour this sauce over the chops and serve.

## ROAST LAMB WITH GARLIC (*Skopové na Česneku*)
### Czechoslovakia

Use leg, loin or shoulder of lamb or mutton in this recipe, and allow about 1½ to 2 hours cooking, depending on the type of joint used. Test frequently as neither lamb nor mutton should be over-cooked as it becomes dry. The best cut for roasting is the leg or shoulder, or the breast, if boned and rolled.

4–6 servings:
2–2½lb (1–1¼kg) lamb or mutton
2–3 garlic cloves
salt to taste
2oz (60g, 4tb) dripping
1 onion, peeled and sliced
½oz (15g, 2tb) flour

Wipe the meat and trim off surplus fat. Mash the garlic, the quantity is a matter of choice, and spread it over the meat. Lightly sprinkle with salt. Heat the dripping in a baking pan on top of the stove, add the onion and fry it very lightly. Add the meat and 3 to 4 tablespoons warm water. Bake in a moderate oven (350°F: 180°C: Gas 4) until tender, basting frequently. When tender, take meat from the oven, put on a hot dish and keep hot. On top of the stove bring the gravy in the baking pan to the boil, sprinkle with flour, stirring all the time, and let it brown. Add a little more water to make a thick gravy, cook for 5 minutes, rub through a sieve and serve separately.

## VIENNESE LAMB RAGOÛT (*Wiener Lammragout*)    Austria

Only good quality dried beans are suitable for this recipe.

4–6 servings:
2lb (1kg) shoulder lamb
1lb (½kg, 3cups) dried white beans
peppercorns to taste
1½oz (45g, 3tb) fat
½lb (250g) onions, peeled and chopped
1 garlic clove, peeled and crushed
pinch each of thyme and marjoram
salt to taste
2tb tomato paste

Soak beans overnight in cold water. Drain well and cook in fresh water with a few peppercorns until they are almost tender. Heat the fat, add the lamb and brown it well. Add the onions, garlic, herbs, salt and tomato paste. Stir well. Drain the beans and add to the pan with enough of their liquid to cover the meat. Continue cooking until the meat is tender and the beans are soft. Just before serving, take the meat from the pan, cut into serving pieces and place on a hot dish. Cover with the beans and gravy and serve with a green salad or cooked green vegetables.

### LAMB STEW (1) (*Bàràny paprikàs*)   Hungary

Stews play a large role in Hungarian cooking. For many it is the staple dish and numerous stews are prepared with the cheapest cuts of meat, even scraps, with the help of dripping, onions and the national condiment, paprika pepper. To thicken the gravy, tomato paste or thick fresh or sour cream is added. Both the tomato paste and cream counteract the somewhat sharp flavour of the paprika.

4 servings:

2lb (1kg) lamb or mutton

1oz (30g,2tb) lard or shortening

2–3 slices fat bacon, diced

¾lb (375g) onions, peeled and sliced

2tsp paprika pepper

2tsp vinegar

salt to taste

¼pt (1dl,⅔cup) fresh or sour cream

½oz (15g,1tb) butter or other fat

Cut the meat into stew-size pieces. Heat the lard, add the bacon and fry this until its fat begins to run. Add the onions and cook until they begin to soften, then add half the paprika, all the vinegar and the meat. Cook the meat until it begins to brown, stirring from time to time, then add salt and enough warm water to cover. Stew gently for about 1 hour or until the meat is tender. Add the cream just before serving. Immediately before serving, heat the butter in a small pan, add the remaining paprika, stir it well, then add 1 to 2 teaspoons warm water and pour this mixture over the stew without further stirring. This gives the stew the coveted red colour and flavour so important to Hungarians. This last-minute butter and paprika addition is usually made for all Hungarian stews.

### LAMB STEW (2) (*Bàràny pörkölt*)   Hungary

A *pörkölt* is prepared in the same manner as the previous lamb stew recipe but tomato pulp, in the same quantity, is used instead of cream to thicken the sauce. *Pörkölts* are made with all varieties of meat and poultry.

## PORK AND VEGETABLES STEYR STYLE
### (*Steirisches Gemüsefleisch*)   Austria

4 servings:
2lb (1kg) shoulder or shoulder butt of pork
1lb (½kg) onions
1 small head celery
2 large carrots
1 parsnip
1 large leek
1–2 potatoes
1 bay leaf
1tb mild vinegar
salt, peppercorns to taste

Wipe the meat with a cloth and cut into stew-sized pieces. Put into a large
pan. Clean all the vegetables (peel the root vegetables), and cut them into
fairly small pieces. Add to the pan with the bay leaf, vinegar, salt, peppercorns and plenty of water. Bring gently to the boil, lower the heat and
cook gently until the meat is very tender, 1½ to 2 hours depending on the
quality of the meat.

Serve the meat with the vegetables.

## PORK WITH HORSERADISH (*Wiener Krenfleisch*)   Austria

4 servings:
2lb (1kg) shoulder or shoulder butt of pork or breast
1 carrot, peeled and sliced
1 celery stalk, chopped
1 small parsnip, peeled and chopped
salt to taste
grated horseradish to taste
1lb (½kg) potatoes

Wash the meat, pat it dry and drop into a large pan with plenty of water. Add the remaining ingredients except the potatoes and bring gently to the boil. Lower the heat and continue to cook gently until the meat is very tender, 1½ to 2 hours. Wash, peel and slice the potatoes and add them to the pan 30 to 40 minutes before the meat is ready.

At this stage the meat can be taken out of the pan, sliced and arranged in a deep serving dish with the vegetables and most of the cooking liquid, then it is simply *Gekochtes Schweinefleisch*, or boiled pork. But if the pork is served with plenty of freshly grated horseradish it then becomes indeed one of Vienna's favourite dishes.

Ribs of boiled beef are served in the same manner and also called *Wiener Krenfleisch*, as is another dish of boiled belly of pork, pigs' trotters, part of the head, ears, etc cooked until tender then sliced, sprinkled with freshly grated horseradish and served with boiled potatoes.

## ROAST PORK (*Vepřová Pečeně*)   Czechoslovakia

4–6 servings:
2–2½lb (1–1¼kg) shoulder or shoulder butt of pork
salt, caraway seeds to taste

Wipe the meat with a damp cloth and, if it is very fat, nick the skin slightly. Rub it all over with salt, place in a baking pan, meaty side down, and sprinkle with caraway seeds. Add a little water to the pan, cover and bake in a moderate oven (350°F: 180°C: Gas 4) for 1 hour. Take the pork from the oven, score the skin into squares, return it to the oven and continue roasting until the pork is tender and the skin crisp and brown. Baste frequently to ensure gentle browning. Roasting time will be 2 to 2½ hours.

Take the pork from the pan, put aside but keep hot. Scrape the baking pan, add a little warm water to the gravy, stir, bring to the boil on top of the stove, rub through a sieve and pour into a sauceboat.

Roast pork, considered one of the Czech national dishes, is served with **dumplings, potatoes and sauerkraut.**

POT ROASTED PORK (*Vepřová Pečeně*)   Czechoslovakia

The best cuts for this recipe would be leg, loin or spare ribs in one piece.

4 servings:
1½lb (¾kg) pork, without bone
1oz (30g,2tb) fat
1 small onion, coarsely chopped
1lb (½kg) carrots
½oz (15g,2tb) flour

Wipe the meat with a damp cloth. Heat the fat, add the onion and gently fry until brown all over. Add the pork (in one piece) and fry until it is brown on one side, then turn and brown the other side. Add enough lightly salted warm water to cover. Cook gently, covered, until the meat is tender. Wash and peel the carrots and cut into thin strips. Add to the pan and continue cooking until these are tender. Dredge with flour, stir gently but well, then add enough warm water to make a fairly thick sauce. Continue cooking a few minutes until the flour loses its raw flavour.

Cut the meat into serving portions and serve on a hot dish garnished with the carrots and the sauce.

Serve with boiled potatoes, potato dumplings or potato cakes.

## PORK CHOPS WITH CARAWAY SEEDS
(*Vepřová Pěcené na Kmíně*)   Czechoslovakia

6 servings:
6 pork chops
salt to taste
1oz (30g,2tb) fat
caraway seeds to taste
flour, for sprinkling

Wipe the chops with a damp cloth, beat gently with a cutlet bat and nick round the edges to prevent curling. Rub lightly with salt. Heat the fat in a large frying pan, add the chops and fry quickly until brown on both sides.

Add a little water, sprinkle with caraway seeds and cook gently until tender. Sprinkle with flour, add about 1 cupful warm water and continue cooking for 5 minutes. Take the chops from the pan and place on a hot plate. Stir the gravy and pour through a sieve over the chops.

Serve with rice, noodles, dumplings or potatoes.

### PORK CHOPS DEBRECEN STYLE
(*Debreceni sertèsborda*)   Hungary

4–6 servings:
4–6 pork chops
½oz (15g,1tb) fat
1 medium-sized onion, peeled and sliced
paprika pepper to taste
4 peppercorns     juice of small lemon

Heat the fat and fry the onion until it begins to change colour. Sprinkle lightly (or generously) with paprika pepper. Add the chops, peppercorns, lemon juice and just enough warm water to prevent sticking. Cover the pan and cook over a low heat until the chops are tender. Check from time to time whether a little more hot water is needed.

Serve with cabbage or sauerkraut and boiled potatoes.

### ROAST SUCKING PIG (*Gebratenes Spanferkel*)   Austria

4–6 servings:
1 sucking pig, about 3 weeks old
salt, pepper to taste
caraway seeds to taste
marjoram, chopped, to taste
a little soft brown sugar
1 lemon
1½oz (45g,3tb) butter
½pt (¼l,1cup) beer for basting (approx)
1 apple

Wipe the piglet inside and out. Rub with salt, pepper (preferably freshly ground), caraway seeds, marjoram and a little brown sugar. Put a lemon or a small piece of smooth wood into its mouth. Wrap the ears and the tail in foil to prevent burning while roasting. Rub the bottom of a large baking pan with about one-third of the butter, spread the rest over the piglet. Place the piglet on the rack of a baking pan on its back with the legs uppermost. Start roasting in a hot oven (400°F: 200°C: Gas 6) for the first 10 minutes, then lower the heat to 350°F (180°C: Gas 4) and continue cooking for 1 hour. If the piglet is roasted in too hot an oven its skin will blister. However, if this does happen, break the blisters with a needle. Baste frequently with beer and the gravy from the pan. Turn the piglet after the first hour of cooking, baste again and continue roasting and basting for another hour. The piglet must be well done, test by twisting the legs. If they seem ready to come from the body, the piglet is tender.

The piglet can be served whole and carved at the table, the lemon or wood replaced by an apple. Or it can be cut into chunks rather than any attempt at slicing and placed on the serving plate and then reshaped into as near as possible its original form.

Bread dumplings usually are served with roast sucking pig, which is considered a festive dish. Any vegetables can be served with it if they are not too strongly flavoured.

## TRANSYLVANIAN PORK AND CABBAGE CASSEROLE
### (*Kolozsvàri káposzta*)   Hungary

This and the following recipe (Ham and Potato Pie) are both of Saxon origin. The Saxons have lived in settlements in Transylvania since the Middle Ages. Kolozsvàr (Cluj or Klausenburg) is the capital of this ancient and beautiful stretch of country which for some time now has been part of Rumania.

4–6 servings:
2lb (1kg) lean boiling pork
2oz (60g,4tb) pork fat
2lb (1kg) sauerkraut
1 large red onion
1oz (30g,2tb) lard or shortening
1½tb paprika pepper
salt to taste
4oz (125g,½cup) rice, long grain
6 thinly sliced strips fat bacon
½pt (¼l,1¼cups) fresh or sour cream, or yogurt

Heat the pork fat in a large pan. Add the sauerkraut, pull the shreds apart if using canned as it is tightly packed in the can. Cook gently for 30 to 40 minutes. Cut the pork into pieces as small as possible. Peel and coarsely chop the onion. Heat the lard, add the onion and cook until it begins to change colour. Add 1 teaspoon paprika pepper and the salt. Add the meat, stir well and cover with water. Cook gently for about 45 minutes or until the meat is quite tender. Cook the rice separately in plenty of rapidly boiling salted water until tender. Drain thoroughly.

Cover the bottom of a casserole with the strips of fat bacon. Add a layer of sauerkraut, then pork and onion, and rice. Repeat these layers until all the ingredients are used up, the number of layers depends on the size of the casserole. The top layer should be of sauerkraut, and each layer must be well sprinkled with salt and pepper. Stir ½ tablespoon of paprika into the cream and pour this over the top of the sauerkraut.

Bake in a moderate oven (350°F: 180°C: Gas 4) for 30 minutes. Serve with boiled potatoes.

## HAM AND POTATO PIE (*Schinkenkartoffeln*)   Austria

4–6 servings:
½lb (¼kg) cooked ham
2lb (1kg) potatoes
2oz (60g,4tb) butter or other fat
salt, pepper, nutmeg to taste
2 eggs, separated
½pt (¼l,1¼cups) milk
fine breadcrumbs for sprinkling

Wash the potatoes and cook in their skins in lightly salted water until tender. Drain, cool and peel. Cut into medium-thin slices. Rub an 8-inch deep baking dish generously with some of the butter. Put two-thirds of the potatoes on the bottom. Sprinkle with salt, pepper and nutmeg.

Dice or coarsely grind the ham. Beat the egg yolks into the milk. Add salt, pepper and nutmeg. Mix into the ham. Beat the egg whites until stiff and fold into the ham mixture. Spread this over the potatoes in the baking dish and cover with the remaining potatoes. Sprinkle with breadcrumbs and dot with the remaining butter. Bake in a moderate oven (350°F: 180°C: Gas 4) for 25 to 30 minutes. Serve with a green salad.

## APPLES, PEARS AND BACON (*Schnitt und Speck*)   South Germany

4–6 servings:
1lb (½kg) apples
1lb (½kg) pears
sugar to taste
6–12 slices lean bacon

The fruit should not be too ripe. Peel the fruit, cut into quarters and discard cores and pips. Put into a pan with water, a little sugar and the bacon. Cover and cook gently until the fruit is soft but still firm.

Serve the fruit in a deep bowl with the liquid and cover with the bacon. If preferred, the bacon can be coarsely chopped. Allow one or two slices for each person.

## MEAT LOAF (*Sekaná*)  Czechoslovakia

The meat for this recipe can be either half beef and pork or a mixture of
beef, pork and veal. Most Czech recipes combine beef and pork, not all
use veal.

4–6 servings:

1½lb (¾kg) ground or minced meat

3 bread rolls

1½oz (45g,3tb) lard or other fat

2–3 thin slices bacon, diced

1 medium-sized onion, peeled and finely chopped

2 eggs, separated

salt, pepper to taste

pinch of dry marjoram

1tsp grated lemon rind

1tb lemon juice

1½oz (45g,1cup) soft breadcrumbs

Soak the bread rolls in water until soft, then squeeze dry. Mix the meats.
Heat one-third of the lard, fry the bacon until the fat runs, drain and mix
into the meat. In the same fat fry the onion until soft and add to the meat.
Mix and knead well. Beat the egg yolks, add to the meat mixture and
knead again thoroughly. Add the soaked bread, salt, pepper, marjoram,
lemon rind and juice and enough breadcrumbs to make a firm paste.
Shape into a loaf. Brush all over with the egg whites.

Heat the rest of the lard in a baking pan. Add the meat roll and bake in
a moderate oven (350°F: 180°C: Gas 4) for about 1 hour or until the loaf
is firm and a knife inserted into it comes out clean. The top will be brown
and have a glazed look. Add a little water to the pan from time to time
but not enough to soak into the loaf and make it soggy.

Thickly slice to serve with potatoes, sauerkraut or with a fruit compôte
(see page 183). While it might seem curious to serve a meat loaf with a
fruit compôte, it is no more curious than serving apple sauce with roast
pork, gooseberry sauce with mackerel, or cranberry or redcurrant jelly
with hare.

## 'SLOPPY' CABBAGE (*Lucskoskàposzta*)   Hungary

4–6 servings:
1lb (½kg) each lean beef and pork
2 small, firm white cabbages
salt, pepper to taste
green herbs, mixed, to taste
parsley, coarsely chopped, to taste
1tb wine vinegar
¼pt (1dl,⅔cup) sour or fresh cream

Wash and dry the meats and put into a pan with plenty of water, bring to a gentle boil and cook gently for about 1 hour. Trim the cabbages, discard any bruised leaves and cut off thick stalks. Cut each cabbage into wedges, 4 to 6 depending on their size. Add these to the pan on top of the meat and cook until tender but not soft.

Take the cabbage from the pan. Press out all the liquid and arrange the cabbage in a baking dish. Cut the beef and pork into medium-sized serving pieces, add to the cabbage, add salt, pepper, herbs, parsley and enough of the stock in which the meat and cabbage was cooked to cover. Add the vinegar and cook in a moderate oven (350°F: 180°C: Gas 4) for about 30 minutes. Just before serving, add the cream and stir well.

Serve with mashed potatoes.

## BRAWN SET IN A PLATE (*Tellersulz*)   South Germany

4–6 servings:
2oz (60g,2envelopes) gelatine
2pt (1l,5cups) clear meat stock
1tb vinegar
2tb white wine
1½lb (¾kg) cold cooked meat, mixed
3 eggs, hard-boiled
1–2 carrots, cooked

In Germany aspic jelly is usually prepared with gelatine leaves. Most makers of gelatine give precise instructions for using their products. However, it is most important the gelatine is completely dissolved. Put it into a cup and fill with cold stock. Place the cup over a pan of hot water and stir the gelatine until it has completely dissolved. Bring the rest of the stock, vinegar and wine to the boil, add the dissolved gelatine and stir until the stock is clear. Leave in a cool place until the aspic jelly begins to set.

In the meantime cut the meat into strips. Usually different kinds of pork are used in this recipe. Slice the eggs and cut the carrots into thin rounds. Divide the meat, eggs and carrots into 4 to 6 soup plates and arrange neatly on the bottom of the plate. Cover each portion with aspic jelly and leave in a cold place, ie the refrigerator, until set.

Turn out to serve with roast potatoes in their jackets or rye bread. A useful summer luncheon dish.

In Hungary a similar dish is prepared with pork but gelatine is not used, instead the liquid jells of its own accord. The brawn should be firm and yet slightly tremble when turned out but naturally keeping its shape. Hungarians serve it either sprinkled with lemon or vinegar, or with freshly grated horseradish.

## KIDNEY AND MUSHROOMS (*Vese Gombàval*)   Hungary

4 servings:
¾lb (375g) calf's kidneys
1lb (½kg) mushrooms
2oz (60g,4tb) lard
1 small onion, peeled and finely chopped
2tsp flour
salt, paprika pepper to taste
¼pt (1dl,⅔cup) cream or white wine

Plunge the kidneys into boiling water, drain at once and pull off the skin which surrounds them. Split them open, remove the membrane and fat and slice, not too thinly or they will toughen. Wash the mushrooms and thinly slice, caps and stems.

Heat the fat in a shallow pan, add the onion, let it cook for 5 minutes, no longer, then add the mushrooms. Cook for a few minutes, add the kidneys and cook gently until the mushrooms are soft and the kidneys fried. Sprinkle the flour, salt and paprika over the top, mix thoroughly but gently, add the cream and continue cooking over a low heat, stirring all the time until the sauce has thickened.

Serve with toast, mashed potatoes or rice.


## CRACKLINGS (*Töpörtyü*)   Hungary

Cracklings are used in many Hungarian and Central European prepara-tions and are made from pork or goose fat. Great chunks of hard fat are cut off slaughtered over-fed geese and pigs. This is rendered down to make cooking fat, also *töpörtyü* or cracklings.

Pork fat is usually available in delicatessen stores, both the Hungarian and German varieties. Sometimes the Hungarian is flavoured with paprika.

4–6 servings:

1lb (½kg) pork fat

2–3tb milk

2–3tb water

Cut off and discard the fat skin. Chop the fat into dice. Put into a pan, add the milk and water and cook over a moderate heat. The milk and water prevents the fat from sticking or burning, also it helps in its browning. When the diced fat is quite brown and all its fat has been rendered, take it from the pan with a perforated spoon. With the back of a wooden spoon, press down the cracklings to remove excess fat but do not press them so hard that they are quite free from fat or they will have no more flavour than wood shavings. The fat in the pan should be left until it is firm and used later for frying.

Cracklings are used to flavour dumplings and can also be nibbled before dinner with drinks. I read of an old Hungarian who was so fond of cracklings he believed angels were given them every morning for breakfast.

# VEGETABLES

### ASPARAGUS WITH A BUTTER SAUCE (*Spargel in Butter Tunke*)
### South Germany

For sauce:

| 4 servings: | 2oz (60g,4tb) butter |
|---|---|
| 2lb (1kg) asparagus | 1oz (30g,4tb) flour |
| 1tsp salt | salt to taste |
| 1tsp sugar | 1 egg |

For this recipe the Germans use the very thick white asparagus. Cut off the woody ends and scrape as far as the purple portion of the stalks. Tie round both ends to make a neat bundle and place upright in a tall, preferably narrow, pan of boiling water. Add the salt and sugar. Cover and cook for about 20 minutes or until the tops are tender—test carefully with a fork to see. Take the asparagus from the pan with equal care, for the tips break easily if roughly treated, drain and place on an oval flat dish.

While the asparagus is cooking, make the sauce. Heat the butter, add the flour and stir to a roux. Add salt to taste and take about 1 cupful of the asparagus liquid from the pan, enough to make a fairly loose sauce that is neither thick nor thin. Gradually add this to the roux, stirring all the while and cook for 10 minutes. Beat the egg. Take the pan from the stove, add the egg and beat the sauce thoroughly. Pour the sauce over the asparagus and serve hot.

## BRUSSELS SPROUTS WITH BUTTER AND BREADCRUMBS
*(Kelbimbò vajasmorzsàval)* Hungary

4–6 servings:
2lb (1kg) Brussels sprouts
salt to taste
3oz (90g,6tb) butter
4oz (125g,2½cups) soft breadcrumbs

Prepare the sprouts by pulling off any damaged outer leaves. Cut a thin slice off the bottom and cut a cross to speed up cooking. Wash the sprouts in plenty of cold water and cook them covered in boiling salted water until just tender, about 15 minutes. Drain thoroughly. Heat the butter in another pan, add the breadcrumbs and fry these until they are brown. Add the sprouts, turn them round and about until coated with the breadcrumbs and butter and serve hot.

## BAVARIAN CABBAGE *(Bayerisches Kraut)* South Germany

The cabbage as a vegetable is almost honoured in Bavaria and the best, so it is said, comes from Ismanning, north of Munich. And many are the lucky housewives living on the route of the lorries' daily morning drive from Ismanning to the *Gross Markthalle* who find a fallen cabbage delivered right to the doorstep.

4–6 servings:
2lb (1kg) large white cabbage
1oz (30g,2tb) pork or chicken fat
1 large onion, peeled and finely chopped
1tb brown sugar
½pt (¼l,1¼cups) white wine
salt, pepper to taste

Wash the cabbage, discard the bruised and broken leaves and thick stalks. Cut into quarters and shred finely.

Heat the fat in a large pan, add the onion and lightly fry until it begins to change colour. Add the sugar, stir it well into the onion, add the wine, cabbage, salt and pepper. Cover and cook over a low heat until the cabbage is tender, at least 1 to 1½ hours.

Serve with roast pork, or goose with chestnuts.

## BOHEMIAN CABBAGE (*Červené zelí*)   Czechoslovakia

4–6 servings:
2lb (1kg) large white cabbage
salt, pepper to taste
½–1tsp caraway seeds
1 small onion, peeled and finely chopped
¼pt (1dl,⅔cup) sour cream

Trim and wash the cabbage, discarding bruised leaves and thick stalks. Cut into quarters and shred finely. Put the cabbage into a large pan, add salt, pepper, caraway seeds, onion and just enough water to cover the bottom of the pan to prevent burning. Cover pan and cook over a low heat until the cabbage is tender. Just before serving, add the cream, stir and continue cooking until the cream is hot.

Serve with boiled pork or ham.

## MORAVIAN CABBAGE (*Zelí po moravsku*)

4–6 servings:
2lb (1kg) large white cabbage
salt to taste
1tsp caraway seeds
1oz (30g,2tb) bacon or pork fat
2–3 slices fat bacon, diced
1 large onion, peeled and finely chopped
½oz (15g,2tb) flour
½oz (15g,1tb) sugar
¼pt (1dl,⅔cup) wine and vinegar mixed

Wash the cabbage and discard bruised leaves and thick stalks. Cut the cabbage into quarters and finely shred. Put into a bowl, add salt and caraway seeds. Leave until required.

Heat the fat in a large pan, add the bacon and fry until it begins to crispen. Add the onion and fry until a golden brown. Sprinkle the flour over the onions, stir and cook for 1 minute. Take the pan from the stove, add 1 cupful of cold water, stirring all the time. When this is smoothly mixed into the onion, add 1 cupful of hot water. Beat until smooth, then add the sugar and wine and vinegar. Return the pan to the heat, bring it gently to the boil, add the cabbage, stir it well into the sauce and cook until tender, 15 to 20 minutes.

The cabbage can be served with boiled ham or pork but also as a main dish garnished with sour cream or yogurt, or with potatoes. A large, tart apple, peeled and diced, is often added to the pan at the same time as the cabbage.

## CABBAGE ROLLS (*Kapustové závitky*)  Czechoslovakia

4–6 servings:
2lb (1kg) firm white cabbage
2 bread rolls
$\frac{1}{4}$pt (1dl,$\frac{2}{3}$cup) milk, wine or water
1lb ($\frac{1}{2}$kg) minced or ground pork
1 large egg
1 small onion, peeled and finely chopped
1–2 slices bacon, diced
salt, pepper to taste
$\frac{1}{2}$tsp ground ginger
2oz (60g,4tb) lard or pork fat

Soak the bread rolls until soft in milk, wine or water. Squeeze the bread until dry. Mix with the pork. Beat the egg, add to the pork mixture then add the onion, bacon, salt, pepper and ginger. Knead well and put aside.

Trim the cabbage, discarding any tough outer leaves and thick stalks. Put the cabbage into a pan of boiling water and cook until the leaves are just soft, about 5 minutes. Take from the pan and drain well. Separate the leaves carefully, one by one, cutting them from the base with a small sharp knife. Spread the leaves out on the kitchen table and carefully thin down the centre vein of each leaf, or flatten gently with a cutlet bat. In the centre of each leaf place about a tablespoon of the pork stuffing. Fold the sides of each leaf over the stuffing, then roll. If the rolls do not seem secure, tie them lightly with thread.

Heat the fat in a large frying pan. Fry the cabbage rolls until lightly brown on both sides. Remove the thread (if using) and place the rolls in a shallow, preferably glass, ovenproof baking dish. They can be fairly tightly packed as they will shrink during cooking. Add enough water to come half-way up the sides of the dish, cover and cook for $1\frac{1}{2}$ to 2 hours in a moderate oven (350°F: 180°C: Gas 4). When the liquid in the dish begins to boil, lower the heat. The rolls can be served in the casserole in which they are cooked.

They are served usually with sour cream or with yogurt used as a sauce, and with boiled potatoes.

### WHITE CABBAGE PANCAKE (*Kelkàposztafasirt*)   Hungary

4–6 servings:
2lb (1kg) white cabbage
1 bread roll
3tb (4tb) milk
1 garlic clove
$1\frac{1}{2}$oz (45g,3tb) butter or other fat
2 eggs, well beaten
2tb breadcrumbs
salt, pepper to taste
oil for frying (see method)

Soak the bread roll in the milk. Wash the cabbage and discard all bruised leaves and hard stalks. Cut into quarters and shred. Cook with the whole garlic in boiling salted water until soft. Drain, discard the garlic. Heat the butter, add the cabbage and cook over a low heat until the cabbage is dry. Squeeze the bread roll until dry and mash until free from lumps. Combine with the eggs, breadcrumbs, salt and pepper. Mix these ingredients into the cabbage mixture. Heat a little oil, just enough to cover the bottom of the pan. Add the cabbage mixture and spread it out like a large, thick pancake. Fry until brown, first on one side then on the other.

Turning the cabbage pancake can be difficult. It is simpler to put the frying pan under the grill (broiler) to brown the top. Serve cut into wedges like a cake.

Cabbage pancake can be served as a main dish with a tomato or mushroom sauce, thick sour cream, or yogurt, or with stewed apples or pears.

## SAUERKRAUT WITH APPLES (*Sauerkraut mit Apfeln*)
### South Germany

This recipe happens to be German but it is a dish one finds throughout Central Europe. When available, use fresh sauerkraut. If using canned, pull it apart with a fork as it is packed tightly.

4–6 servings:
2lb (1kg) sauerkraut
4 large tart apples
1oz (30g,2tb) pork dripping
1 small onion, peeled and finely chopped
1tsp sugar
1 potato
1tb flour
salt, pepper, caraway seeds to taste

Melt the fat in a large pan, add the onion and gently fry for 3 to 4 minutes. Add the sauerkraut and fry for 2 minutes. Add boiling water to cover. Peel and slice the apples, add to the pan. Sprinkle with sugar, cover the pan and cook very slowly for 45 minutes. Peel and chop the potato. Take enough liquid from the pan to mix with the flour to a thin paste. Stir the paste into the pan with the chopped potato, add salt, pepper and caraway seeds and cook a further 10 minutes.

Serve with Vienna or Frankfurter sausages, or other similar continental-style sausages, particularly *Bratwurst*.

## CARROTS COOKED IN BUTTER (*Pàrolt sàrgarèpa*) Hungary

4 servings:
1lb (½kg) carrots
2oz (60g,4tb) butter or other fat
2tb parsley, finely chopped
1tsp sugar
salt to taste
½oz (15g,2tb) flour
½pt (¼l,1¼cups) clear stock or water

Use only young and tender carrots for this recipe. Wash and scrape the carrots and cut into medium-thin slices—about ¼ inch thick. Over a low heat melt the butter in a pan, add the carrots and stir well until coated with butter. Add the parsley, sugar and salt. Cover the pan and continue to cook over a low heat until the carrots are soft, shaking the pan or stirring from time to time to prevent burning.

While the carrots are cooking, prepare a thick sauce. Mix the flour with enough of the stock to make a thin paste. Pour the rest of the liquid into a small pan, bring gently to the boil and add the flour-and-stock paste, stirring all the time. Continue cooking until the sauce is boiling, lower the heat and cook for 5 minutes. Pour this sauce over the carrots, stir well but gently and continue cooking for a few minutes longer.

Serve with boiled meats or poultry.

## BAKED CAULIFLOWER (*Rakott karfiol*) Hungary

4–6 servings:
1 large cauliflower
salt to taste
½oz (15g,1tb) fat for greasing
fine breadcrumbs, for sprinkling
½ cup buttered breadcrumbs (see page 23)
2 eggs      ½oz (15g,2tb) flour
1pt (½l,2½cups) sour or fresh cream
1–2 thick slices cooked ham, chopped

Trim cauliflower, discard tough stalks and place the whole head in cold salted water. Leave for 30 minutes to dislodge dust and any insects. Drain and cook in boiling salted water until just tender but still firm. Rub a baking dish with the fat and lightly sprinkle with fine breadcrumbs.

While the cauliflower is cooking, make the buttered breadcrumbs. Next, separate the eggs, lightly beat the yolks and mix with the flour. Blend in the cream. Beat the egg whites until stiff and, using a metal spoon, fold into the egg mixture. Drain cauliflower and break into small flowerets. Fit half of these neatly into the greased baking dish. Sprinkle the ham over the top and spread with half the egg mixture. Arrange the remaining cauliflower over the top then spread with remaining egg mixture, sprinkle with buttered breadcrumbs and bake in a moderate oven (350°F: 180°C: Gas 4) for about 20 minutes or until the top is lightly browned.

Instead of buttered, fine breadcrumbs can be used, dotted with butter.

## DEEP FRIED CAULIFLOWER IN A SOUR CREAM SAUCE
*Kiràntott karfiol tejfölös màrtàssal)*   Hungary

4–6 servings:
1 large white cauliflower
fat, for deep frying
2 whole eggs
2tb (2½tb) milk
fine breadcrumbs, for sprinkling

For sauce:

2 egg yolks, lightly beaten
½pt (¼l,1¼cups) sour or fresh cream
2tsp lemon juice
salt, pepper to taste
1tsp paprika pepper

Trim the cauliflower, removing bruised leaves and the hard, woody stalks. Break into 4 to 6 large flowerets. Steep in cold water with a little salt to remove any dust or small insects. Leave for about 30 minutes then drain and cook in boiling salted water until tender but still firm.

Prepare the sauce. Combine the egg yolks, cream, lemon juice, salt, pepper and paprika. Beat well and pour into the top of a double boiler. Cook over simmering water, stirring all the time, until thick. Put aside but keep warm.

Heat plenty of fat or oil for deep frying; remember this takes some time to heat so start preparing this at least 15 minutes before the cauliflower is cooked.

Drain the cauliflower and let it cool slightly. Beat the whole eggs into the milk. Season the breadcrumbs with salt and pepper. When the fat is boiling, dip the cauliflower first into the beaten eggs, then into the breadcrumbs. Deep fry, 1 or 2 flowerets at a time depending on the size of the pan. When the cauliflower is a golden brown drain carefully on kitchen paper, place in a deep serving dish, pour the sauce over the top and serve at once.

If served as a main dish, it is only sufficient for 4 servings.


## PURÉE OF CELERIAC (*Püree von Sellerie*)    Austria

4–6 servings:
1½lb (¾kg) celeriac (see page 23)
3oz (90g,6tb) butter or other fat
salt to taste
¼tsp black pepper
½pt (¼l,1¼cups) vegetable stock or water
½oz (15g,2tb) flour
¼pt (1dl,⅔cup) fresh or sour cream

Peel the celeriac and cut into quarters and then into cubes. Heat the butter, add the celeriac, salt, pepper and half the stock or water. Cover and cook until the celeriac is soft and all the liquid has evaporated. Sprinkle with flour, add the remaining liquid, bring to the boil and cook for another 10 minutes or until the flour is cooked and has lost its aroma. Rub through a sieve or purée in a blender, return the purée to the pan, add the cream, stir and serve.

It is difficult to say how long celeriac takes to cook, 20 to 60 minutes and sometimes even longer—it depends on its age. (If the celeriac takes a long time to cook then extra liquid will be required.)


## DEEP FRIED MUSHROOMS (*Gebackene Champignons*)  Austria

For this dish very fresh, large open mushrooms are required, preferably all about the same size.

6 servings:
3lb (1½kg) mushrooms
salt, pepper to taste
cooking oil (see method)
flour, for coating
2 eggs, well beaten
fine breadcrumbs, for coating

For this recipe I suggest if possible either a mild-flavoured olive oil or groundnut oil which has almost no flavour. A too strongly flavoured oil will spoil the flavour of the mushrooms.

Wash the mushrooms and gently pat them dry. Cut off their stems, these can be used to flavour another dish. If the mushrooms are very large, cut into wide strips; smaller mushrooms are best left whole. Sprinkle the undersides with salt and pepper.

Have ready plenty of hot oil in a deep large pan with a frying basket. Dip the mushrooms first in flour, then in beaten egg and finally in bread-crumbs. Place in the frying basket and lower this gently into the hot oil. Fry the mushrooms briefly until they become golden and serve at once on hot plates.

Serve either as a main course for luncheon or as a hot hors d'oeuvre with a tartare sauce in which case it can perhaps serve 8.

## STEWED MUSHROOMS (*Dušené houby*)   Czechoslovakia

6 servings:
2lb (1kg) mushrooms
2oz (60g,4tb) butter or other fat
2–3tb parsley, finely chopped
salt, pepper to taste
1tsp caraway seeds
½oz (15g,1tb) flour
¼pt (1dl,⅔cup) red or white wine
¼pt (1dl,⅔cup) sour or fresh cream (optional)

Wash the mushrooms and slice thickly or thinly, as preferred. Heat the butter in a shallow pan, add the mushrooms, parsley, salt, pepper and caraway seeds. Cook gently for 15 to 20 minutes. Combine the flour with a little of the wine to make a thin paste and stir it well into the fat until the mixture is smooth. Add the rest of the wine and sour cream, if using, stir well and continue cooking for another 15 minutes, stirring from time to time. Serve as a vegetable or, if preferred, on crisp buttered toast.

## MUSHROOMS WITH EGGS (*Houby s vejci*)   Czechoslovakia

4–6 servings:
1- 1½lb (½–¾kg) mushrooms
¼lb (125g,½cup) fat
1 medium-sized onion, peeled and sliced
1tsp caraway seeds
salt to taste
6 eggs (more if preferred)

Wash the mushrooms and slice thickly or thinly, as preferred. Heat the fat, add the onion and fry until it begins to change colour. Add the caraway seeds and salt, then the mushrooms, lower the heat and cook gently until the mushrooms are tender. Stir from time to time. Lightly beat the eggs, add them to the pan, stirring and cooking until the eggs are set. Serve with potato dumplings (see page 135) or on rounds of toast.

## MUSHROOMS WITH ONION (*Houby na cibulce*)  Czechoslovakia

4-6 servings:
1lb (½kg) mushrooms
1 small onion, finely sliced
2oz (60g, 4tb) butter or other fat
salt to taste
½tsp caraway seeds

Wash, pat dry and thickly slice the mushrooms. Heat the butter and gently fry the onion until it begins to change colour. Add the mushrooms, a little salt and the caraway seeds. Cover the pan and cook over a low heat until the mushrooms are soft, about 25 minutes. Do not add any liquid.

Serve with plain boiled potatoes, preferably floury, or with thick chunks of dark, rather soft bread to mop up the sauce. This can be a slightly indigestible dish so keep the portions small.

## MUSHROOMS WITH SOUR CREAM (*Gombà fözelèk*)  Hungary

4 servings:
1lb (½kg) mushrooms
2oz (60g, 4tb) butter or other fat
1–2 onions, peeled and finely chopped
salt, pepper to taste
1tsp paprika pepper
¾pt (½l, 1pt) fresh or sour cream

Wash and slice the mushrooms thickly or thinly, as preferred. Heat the fat and fry the onions until a golden brown. Add the mushrooms, salt, pepper and about 1 heaped teaspoon paprika pepper. Cover and cook gently until tender. Add the cream, stir well and bring slowly to the boil.

Serve with fried eggs, boiled potatoes or croûtons (see page 43), or on toast.

This and the three preceding mushroom recipes are best if edible fungi, ie *cèpe*, orange-cap, boletus or even field mushrooms are used.

## PURÉE OF GREEN PEAS (*Erbsenpüree*)  Austria

A useful recipe for cooking those hard and often tough peas which come at the end of the season, or the large frozen peas. To obtain 2lb of hulled peas, 3lb of unshelled are required.

4–6 servings:
2lb (1kg) green peas, after hulling
1 small onion, peeled and chopped
salt to taste
sugar to taste
2oz (60g,4tb) butter or other fat
1 egg yolk, well beaten
¼pt (1dl,⅔cup) fresh cream

Cook the peas with the onion in boiling salted water over a brisk heat until very soft. Drain and rub through a sieve. Return them to the pan, add salt and sugar and reheat over a low heat. Add the butter, stirring it well into the peas. Beat the egg yolk into the cream then stir it into the peas. Continue cooking gently until the peas are reheated for if the mixture boils the egg and cream might curdle.

## STUFFED SWEET PEPPERS (*Töltött paprikàs*)  Hungary

3–6 servings:
6 large firm sweet peppers
1oz (30g,2tb) lard or shortening
3oz (90g,⅓cup) rice
2 cups hot water or stock (approx)
1oz (30g,2tb) pork or poultry fat
1tb chopped onion
1tb parsley, finely chopped
½lb (¼kg) minced or ground pork
1 egg, well beaten
salt, pepper to taste
½pt (¼l,1¼cups) thin tomato juice

If possible choose peppers of equal size. Slice off the top of each and put tops aside. Scrape out the seeds and cut away the core. Put the peppers into a bowl and pour boiling water over them. Leave for 15 minutes then drain by leaving them upside-down on a wire rack. This will soften the skins.

In the meantime prepare the filling. Heat the lard, add the rice, cook until it looks transparent then add the hot liquid. When adding the hot liquid to the rice it sizzles alarmingly, so add it gradually. Stir well and bring to the boil. Cook until the rice is tender, about 15 minutes. Drain well. In another pan heat the pork fat, add the onion, parsley and pork. Mix the rice with the egg, add salt and pepper then add the pork and onion mixture.

Fill the peppers loosely with the stuffing (overfilling causes the stuffing to congeal into a hard mass). Replace the pepper tops. Put the peppers into a large shallow pan standing firmly upright otherwise their filling will fall out. Add the tomato juice, there must be sufficient to come halfway up the sides of the peppers; if there is not enough, add a little warm water. Cook over a moderate heat for about 1 hour or until the peppers are tender but still firm.

Stuffed peppers are served alone as a main dish.

## SWEET PEPPERS WITH TOMATOES (*Paprikàs-Paradicsomos lecsò*)
### Hungary

4–6 servings:
2–3 large sweet peppers
3 large firm tomatoes
1 small onion
1½oz (45g, 3tb) lard or shortening
salt, pepper to taste
1–2tsp sugar (optional)

Cut the sweet peppers into thick strips, discarding the core and seeds. Scald the tomatoes by pouring boiling water over them and leaving to stand for a few minutes. Pour off water and they will be easier to peel and thinly slice. Peel and thinly slice the onion. Heat the fat in a pan, add the onion and fry until transparent, add the sweet peppers, simmer for a few minutes then cover with the tomatoes. Add salt, pepper and sugar. Cook gently for 30 to 45 minutes. This slight but pleasant dish is served with omelettes, with scrambled eggs, also with fish and meat.

### TIROLESE FRIED POTATOES (*Tiroler Gröstl*)   Austria

4–6 servings:
2lb (1kg) potatoes
1½oz (45g,3tb) fat
2 large onions, finely chopped
½lb (¼kg) cooked meat, diced
salt, pepper to taste
parsley, chopped, or caraway seeds to garnish

This is a typical country dish; usually pork or poultry fat is used for the frying, and the meat can be any kind of left-over meat, roast or boiled, or diced bacon, or coarsely chopped sausage.

Scrub and cook the potatoes in their jackets, cool, peel and thickly slice. Heat the fat, add the onions and fry until they are soft and golden. Add the meat, fry for a few minutes, then add the potatoes and mix them well into the mixture. Let them cook until the potatoes begin to brown, they should not be as dark as for sauté potatoes. Add salt and pepper, sprinkle with parsley or caraway seeds and serve hot.

In the Tirol they serve a gherkin, tomato or green salad with this dish.

### PAPRIKA POTATOES (*Paprikàs burgonya*)   Hungary

3 servings:
1lb (½kg) potatoes
1oz (30g,2tb) pork or bacon fat
1 medium-sized onion, peeled and chopped
2tsp paprika pepper
salt, pepper to taste
¼pt (1dl,⅔cup) fresh or sour cream

Wash and peel the potatoes and cut into thick slices or quarters. Heat the fat in a pan, add the onion and cook slowly until soft and transparent. Add the paprika, salt and pepper and mix thoroughly. Take the pan from the heat, add the cream, stir this well into the onion, then add the potatoes. Cover the pan and cook over a low heat until the potatoes are tender, 30 to 35 minutes. Do not let the potatoes brown and from time to time turn them over gently.

Instead of cream, tomato purée or sauce can be used, also a clove of garlic often is added, and caraway seeds. It is a question of taste.

## NEW POTATOES IN A CREAM SAUCE (*Tejfeles ujburgonya*)
### Hungary

4–6 servings:
2lb (1kg) new potatoes
3oz (90g, 6tb) butter or other fat
1 egg yolk
¼pt (1dl, ⅔cup) fresh cream
parsley, or chives, finely chopped for sprinkling

Wash the potatoes and cook without peeling in boiling salted water until tender. Drain and peel as soon as possible. While the potatoes are cooking, beat two-thirds of the butter until soft, add the egg yolk and continue beating until the mixture is like cream. Add the cream and whisk again. Heat the remaining butter in a shallow pan, add the potatoes and toss them lightly until they are reheated and coated with butter. Add the cream sauce, stirring gently all the time to completely cover the potatoes. Simmer until the sauce is hot. Immediately before serving, sprinkle the potatoes with chopped parsley or chives. Serve as a separate dish.

Instead of parsley, mint may be used but not too much as its flavour is strong. Also good, but milder in flavour, are fresh dill and chervil. Firm old potatoes can also be cooked as above.

## POTATOES IN TOMATO SAUCE (*Paradicsomos burgonya*)  Hungary

**Method 1**

4–6 servings:
2lb (1kg) potatoes
2oz (60g,4tb) butter or other fat
1 small onion, peeled and finely chopped
½pt (¼l,1¼cups) tomato juice, fresh or canned
2tsp sugar
pepper to taste
½pt (¼l,1¼cups) fresh or sour cream
¼pt (1dl,⅔cup) milk
2tb parsley, finely chopped

Scrub the potatoes and cook them in their skins in boiling salted water until tender. Drain, cool, peel and thickly slice. Put aside but keep warm. Heat the butter, add the onion and cook until it is soft and begins to change colour. Take the pan from the stove. Add the tomato juice, sugar and pepper, stirring all the time. Combine the cream and the milk and add this little by little to the tomato sauce, stirring all the time. Add the potatoes, mix them gently to avoid breaking them up and return the pan to the stove. Cook over a low heat until the sauce is hot and the potatoes reheated. Do not let the mixture boil or the sauce will curdle.

Immediately before serving, sprinkle with parsley.

**Method 2**

In this recipe no cream is used and the sauce is thickened with a roux.

4–6 servings:
2lb (1kg) potatoes
2oz (60g,4tb) lard or shortening
2 slices fat bacon, diced
1½oz (45g,6tb) flour
1pt (½l,2½cups) tomato juice
salt, pepper to taste
1–2tsp sugar

Cook and slice the potatoes as in method 1. Heat the fat in a pan or casserole, add the bacon and lightly fry until the fat runs and the bacon begins to crispen. Add the flour, stir it well into the fat then, little by little, add the tomato juice, stirring all the while. The sauce should be of medium thickness, therefore a little warm water may also be required, it depends on the quality of the flour and the thickness of the juice. Add salt, pepper and sugar and bring gently to the boil. Add the sliced potatoes, mix gently, lower the heat and simmer until the potatoes are reheated.

Serve hot. Both these potato dishes can be served as a main course as they are very substantial.

## UPTURNED POTATOES (*Gesturzte Kartoffeln*)   Austria

4 servings:
2lb (1kg) waxy potatoes
3oz (90g,6tb) fat
1oz (30g,2tb) butter
fine breadcrumbs, for sprinkling
salt, pepper to taste
large egg, well beaten

Wash the potatoes and cook them in their skins in boiling salted water until tender. Drain, cool, peel and then slice into medium-thick slices. Heat the fat in a large frying pan, add as many slices of potato as it will hold and fry on both sides until beginning to change colour, they should not become even a golden brown except round the edges. Drain on absorbent paper. Repeat this until all the potatoes are fried.

Rub a round casserole or soufflé dish generously with butter and sprinkle lightly all round the inside with breadcrumbs. Arrange the fried potatoes in the casserole in layers, sprinkle with salt and pepper. Add the egg, dot with butter—a little extra can be added, if liked—and bake in a moderate oven (350°F: 180°C: Gas 4) for 25 to 30 minutes or until the top has browned. Turn out to serve.

This dish goes well with creamed mushrooms, fried kidneys, sliced fried bacon, or with cold ham plus a green salad.

## FRIED TOMATO SLICES (*Ràntott Paradicsom*)  Hungary

3–6 servings:
6 large firm tomatoes
2 eggs
salt to taste
fat, for deep frying (see method)
fine breadcrumbs, for coating

Wipe the tomatoes and, without peeling them, cut into thick slices horizontally. Put the slices on a sieve and let the juice drain out. Beat the eggs thoroughly and add salt. Heat plenty of fat or oil in a deep frying pan so that the tomatoes will be covered when cooking. Dip the tomato slices into the beaten egg then into breadcrumbs. At once put into the boiling fat and fry on both sides until brown.

   Serve with meat or as a main dish sprinkled with parsley. Or serve with sour cream or natural yogurt.

## MIXED VEGETABLES (*Lecsò*)  Hungary

This is a dish of mixed local vegetables not unlike the well-known dish *ratatouille* from Provence. Sometimes the *lecsò* is served with eggs, with rice, or with diced bacon and sausages of all kinds, fried or boiled, or pasta. The following is a basic recipe.

4–6 servings:
1½lb (¾kg) tomatoes
1½lb (¾kg) sweet peppers
2oz (60g,4tb) fat
1 large onion, peeled and finely chopped
1 tsp paprika pepper
salt, pepper to taste

Scald the tomatoes (see recipe for Sweet Peppers Stewed with Tomatoes), peel and cut into quarters. Cut each pepper lengthwise into 6 or 8 pieces, discarding the core and seeds. Heat the fat, add the onion and cook this until it begins to change colour and soften. Add the paprika and stir well before adding the sweet peppers and tomatoes. Sprinkle lightly with salt and pepper, cover the pan and cook over a slow heat until the mixture is soft, 30 to 45 minutes.

If adding rice, use about half a cupful to the above quantity of vegetables and add after the tomatoes. Add water to cover, cover the pan and cook until the rice is soft.

Bacon can be diced, the quantity is to taste, and fried with the onions. Well-beaten eggs are often added after the vegetables have been cooking for 30 minutes, cooked gently and stirred from time to time with a fork. They should be thick and creamy but moist.

Although the Hungarians claim this as a dish of Hungarian origin, the Serbs lay claim to it as well, also it is popular in Austria. Some cooks, particularly in Vienna, like to add caraway seeds, also garlic and green herbs such as parsley, basil or dill. It is important it should be served hot, although if cooked in olive oil, which does not congeal, the dish is equally good cold or even tepid. It goes well with sausages of almost all kinds, fried or boiled, or with boiled potatoes, with rice, cooked separately not with it, also it is excellent with pasta.

## HEAVEN AND EARTH (*Himmel und Erde*)    South Germany

4 servings:
1lb ($\frac{1}{2}$kg) potatoes
1lb ($\frac{1}{2}$kg) cooking apples
salt, pepper to taste
4–6 slices fat bacon

Peel the potatoes, cut into quarters and cook in boiling salted water for 10 to 15 minutes. While they are cooking, peel and quarter the apples. Add these to the pan with salt and pepper and continue cooking until both potatoes and apples are tender. Dice the bacon and fry in its own fat until crisp. Drain the potatoes and apples carefully. Serve on a hot dish sprinkled with the fried bacon.

This typical German mixture of fruit and vegetables is served with fried liver, kidneys or sausages, also with grilled or fried pork chops.

### SILESIAN HEAVEN (*Schlesisches Himmelreich*)  South Germany

Those who have not eaten this dish have not learned to live, according to
the Silesians.

4–6 servings:

1lb (½kg) mixed dried fruit—prunes, apples, pears etc.

1lb (½kg) smoked pork

1 onion, peeled and stuck with 2 cloves

2oz (60g,4tb) fat

½oz (15g,1tb) flour

pinch of salt

½oz (15g,1tb) sugar

1tb lemon juice

Soak the fruit overnight in plenty of tepid water. Remove the stones
from the prunes. Put the pork with the onion into a pan, just cover with
water and cook for about 1 hour (do not add more water than to just
cover). Add the fruit with its liquid and continue to cook slowly for 2
hours. Take the meat from the pan, slice and put it aside but keep warm.
Take out the onion and discard. In another fairly large pan melt the fat,
add the flour and stir to a roux. Gradually add the liquid from the meat
and fruit and stir to a sauce. Stir this mixture back into the fruit. Bring
gently to the boil, add salt, sugar and lemon juice and pour the sauce over
the meat.

Serve with dumplings or, if preferred, with small gnocchi-shaped
noodles.

# SAUCES

### ANCHOVY SAUCE (*Sardellensosse*)   Austria

4–6 servings:
6 anchovy fillets in oil
1½oz (45g,3tb) butter
1 small onion, peeled and minced
1tb parsley, finely chopped
1oz (30g,¼cup) flour
½pt (¼l,1¼cups) clear stock
2tb lemon juice
salt, sugar, pepper to taste

Rinse the anchovy fillets under warm water. Finely chop. Heat the butter in a pan, add the anchovies, onion and parsley and cook for about 5 minutes. Sprinkle with flour and stir well. Gradually add the stock, stirring all the time to make a thick sauce. Simmer for 5 minutes. Beat well until the mixture is smooth then add the remaining ingredients and rub through a sieve.

This sauce is served with freshwater fish, also with boiled meats, including tongue. I also serve this sauce with baked spinach dishes, ie Soufflé, Eggs Florentine or Spinach Omelette.

### CHIVE SAUCE (*Schnittlauchsosse*)   Austria

4–6 servings:
¼lb (125g) soft white bread, without crust
4tb milk
3 eggs, hard-boiled
6tb olive oil
1tb white sugar
3tb mild vinegar
1–2tsp continental mustard
3tb chives, finely chopped

Rub the bread into coarse crumbs, mix with the milk and leave until the bread is soft. Shell and chop the eggs, combine with the bread and rub through a coarse sieve. Add the oil drop by drop to make a thick sauce. Add the sugar, vinegar, mustard and, last of all, the chives.

Excellent with fish, especially freshwater fish.

### WARM CHIVE SAUCE (*Meleg metélöhagyma (snidling) màrtàs*) Hungary

4–6 servings:
1oz (30g,2tb) butter or other fat
½oz (15g,2tb) flour
2tb finely chopped chives,
¼pt (1dl,⅔cup) warm water
1tb wine vinegar or lemon juice
salt, pepper to taste
3tb cream

Heat the butter or fat, add the flour and fry until the mixture is smooth and a golden brown. Add the chives, stir well then gradually add the water, stirring all the time until the sauce is thick. Add the vinegar and stir well. Take the pan from the stove, add the salt and pepper and stir in the cream.

Serve warm with boiled meats.

### DILL SAUCE (*Koprová Omáčka*) Czechoslovakia

4–6 servings:
1pt (½l,2½cups) cream
½oz (15g,2tb) flour
salt to taste
1oz (30g,2tb) sugar
2 egg yolks
1tb finely chopped dill
1tb wine vinegar
½oz (15g,1tb) unsalted butter

Instead of cream, rich milk can be used, or half cream and half milk.

Mix the flour with enough of the cream to make a thin paste, then stirring all the time add the rest of the cream, salt and sugar. Pour into a pan, bring gently to the boil then simmer for 15 minutes, stirring all the time. Beat the egg yolks until smooth. Take the pan from the stove and beat in the egg yolks. Do not return the sauce to the stove. In another pan mix the dill with the vinegar and bring to the boil. Beat this into the cream. Immediately before serving, melt the butter and add this to the sauce. Serve hot with fish.

### HORSERADISH SAUCE WITH GRATED APPLE (*Apfelkren*) Austria

4–6 servings:
3tb horseradish, grated
¼pt (1dl,⅔cup) clear stock
1–2 tart apples, peeled and grated
3tb olive oil
1tb wine vinegar
1tsp white sugar
salt, pepper to taste

Bring the stock to the boil. Pour this over the horseradish, stir well then add the remaining ingredients. Serve with boiled meats.

## CREAMED HORSERADISH SAUCE (*Oberskren*)  Austria

4–6 servings:
½pt (¼l,1¼cups) white sauce
1tsp white sugar
¼lb (125g) grated horseradish
¼pt (1dl,⅔cup) thick cream

Prepare the white sauce, add the sugar, the grated horseradish and cream.
Bring gently just to the boil, stirring all the time. Rub through a sieve.
A mild-flavoured sauce to serve with boiled meats.

## HUNTER'S SAUCE (*Jägersosse*)  Austria

4–6 servings:
1oz (30g,2tb) butter
1 small onion, peeled and finely chopped
1oz (30g,¼cup) flour
1tb parsley, finely chopped
½pt (¼l,1¼cups) water
¼pt (1dl,⅔cup) dry white wine
2tb tomato purée
¼lb (125g) mushrooms, finely chopped

Heat the butter, add the onion, let this cook until it begins to soften, then
add the flour and mix well. Add the parsley then gradually the water and
wine, stirring all the time. Add the tomato purée and the mushrooms and
continue cooking, still stirring, for about 8 minutes.

Serve with steaks or roast meat.

## MUSHROOM SAUCE (*Schwammerlsosse*)   Austria

4–6 servings:
½lb (¼kg) mushrooms
1½oz (45g,3tb) butter or other fat
½ small onion, peeled and finely chopped
salt, pepper to taste
1tb lemon juice
1tb finely chopped parsley
½oz (15g,2tb) flour
¼pt (1dl,⅔cup) warm stock or water
¼pt (1dl,⅔cup) cream or milk

Wash the mushrooms, pat them dry and slice the caps and stems. Heat the butter, add the mushrooms, onion, salt, pepper and lemon juice. Sprinkle with parsley. Cover the pan and cook over a gentle heat until the mushrooms are soft. Uncover, stir well, then sprinkle in the flour and stir again. Add the stock and, stirring gently, continue cooking for 10 minutes then add the cream. Continue cooking until this is hot but do not bring the sauce to the boil.

Instead of cream, red or white wine can be used. If lemon is not available, use a mild wine vinegar, dry white wine or beer. This recipe produces a rather thick sauce to serve with meat and chicken.

## PAPRIKA SAUCE (*Paprika màrtàs*)   Hungary

4–6 servings:
2oz (60g,4tb) lard or shortening
1 small onion, peeled and coarsely chopped
1½oz (45g,6tb) flour
1tsp paprika pepper
1tb wine vinegar
salt, pepper to taste
1pt (½l,2½cups) warm stock, or water
¼pt (1dl,⅔cup) tomato juice, or cream

Heat the lard and fry the onion until it begins to soften. Add the flour, stir well then add the paprika, vinegar, salt and pepper. Mix well and little by little add the stock or water and continue cooking and stirring until the sauce is thick. Finally add the tomato juice and stir well. If the sauce is too thick, add more liquid.

Serve the sauce with boiled fish, meats or poultry and boiled sausages. Sausages or potatoes are cooked in paprika sauce and served as a snack in Hungary. If cooking potatoes or sausages in this sauce, add a little extra liquid.

### TOMATO SAUCE (*Paradicsom màrtàs*)   Hungary

6 servings:
2oz (60g,4tb) lard or shortening
1 small onion, peeled and chopped
2–3 parsley sprigs, chopped
2lb (1kg) ripe tomatoes, chopped
1oz (30g,2tb) butter
1oz (30g,4tb) flour
salt, pepper to taste
1tb lemon juice
2tsp (2½tsp) sugar
1–2tb red wine

Heat the lard, add the onion and cook until this begins to soften. Add the parsley, tomatoes and just enough water to moisten the tomatoes until they begin to cook. Cook over a low heat until the tomatoes are very soft. Rub through a fine sieve.

While the tomatoes are cooking, heat the butter, add the flour and cook slowly, stirring continuously to a roux. Add the sieved tomato gradually, stirring all the time to make a thick smooth sauce. Add salt, pepper, lemon juice and sugar and mix thoroughly. Finally stir in the wine.

When tomatoes are scarce, the same quantity of canned tomatoes may be used; the sauce will have just as good a flavour.

Serve with noodles, spaghetti, cold meats, over boiled potatoes, or rice.

## FROTHY WINE SAUCE (*Weinschaumsosse*)    South Germany

4–6 servings:
½pt (¼l, 1¼cups) white wine
2 eggs
2 egg yolks
2tb lemon juice
2oz (60g, ¼cup) fine sugar
1tsp lemon flavoured sugar

Beat all the ingredients thoroughly together in a bowl. Put the bowl over a pan of boiling water but do not let the bottom of the bowl touch the water, and continue beating or whisking until the sauce boils and begins to thicken. Take the sauce from the pan. If it should separate, return it to the pan and continue cooking. The best way to judge whether the sauce is ready is to put a little in a glass, if it remains firm in the glass, then it is ready. Serve with sweet puddings.

## PLUM SAUCE (*Klevera*)    Czechoslovakia

This *klevera* is another example of a recipe repeated in varying forms throughout Central Europe, also spilling over into the Balkans. It is a type of jam or preserve to spread over puddings as a sauce but not intended to keep as a jam. It is not usually made in large quantities.

4–6 servings:
2lb (1kg) plums
½lb (250g, 1cup) preserving or granulated sugar
3tb wine vinegar

Wash the plums, remove and discard the stones and cut the flesh into small pieces. Cook gently until soft but not mushy. Add sugar and vinegar then bring to the boil and continue cooking until the mixture is very thick. Stir from time to time.

The plums must be very juicy and cooked slowly as they are cooked without water. Stir carefully to avoid breaking up the fruit.

# DUMPLINGS and PASTA

## SMALL DUMPLINGS (*Galuska*)   Hungary

4–6 servings:
2oz (60g,4tb) butter
2 eggs
pinch of salt
½lb (250g,2cups) plain flour
½pt (¼l,1cup) milk (approx)

Cream the butter. Beat the eggs and combine with the butter and continue beating until the mixture is light. Add the salt and flour and beat until the mixture is smooth. Gradually add the milk, enough to make a dough neither too thick nor too thin. A little more milk may be required; much depends on the absorbent quality of the flour. Continue beating until blisters begin to appear on the surface of the dough. Dampen a pastry board and turn out the dough on to this. Have ready a large pan with plenty of lightly salted, boiling water. Break off tiny pieces of the dough with a small spoon, a coffee spoon is the ideal size. Drop these at once into the boiling water. Let the dumplings boil until they rise to the surface then take from the pan at once with a perforated spoon. If they remain too long in the water they become soggy and tough. Rinse them in cold water and drain in a colander.

When ready to serve in a soup or stew, throw them for a moment or so into the pan. Or the dumplings can be tossed in a pan of hot butter and served either lightly sprinkled with salt, or with sour cream.


## NOODLES (*Noky*)   Czechoslovakia

These are made in the same manner as the *galuska* and served with meat.


## BREAD DUMPLINGS (*Housekové knedlíčky*)   Czechoslovakia

4–6 servings:
4oz (125g,3cups) soft white breadcrumbs
$\frac{1}{4}$pt (1dl,$\frac{2}{3}$cup) milk
2oz (60g,4tb) butter or other fat
2 egg yolks, well beaten
salt to taste

Soak the breadcrumbs in the milk. Squeeze dry. Soften the butter, add the egg yolks and beat until the mixture is smooth and light. Add salt. Add the breadcrumbs—there must be enough to make a firm dough. Break off small pieces of this mixture and shape these into dumplings. Drop into boiling salted water and cook for a few minutes only or until they rise to the top of the pan. Drain and serve as a soup garnish.


## LIVER DUMPLINGS (*Játrové knedlíčky*)   Czechoslovakia

4–6 servings:
$\frac{1}{2}$lb ($\frac{1}{4}$kg) liver
1 garlic clove
1oz (30g,2tb) butter
salt, pepper to taste
1 egg
6oz (180g,4cups) soft breadcrumbs
flour, for coating

Mince (grind) the liver. Peel, crush and mash the garlic. Beat the butter with a little salt until soft. Add the egg and when well beaten add the liver, pepper and breadcrumbs. Do not add the crumbs all at once; a little less or more may be required, depending on the size of the egg and the softness of the bread. Mix everything together to make a thick paste or dough. With floured hands, break off pieces of the liver mixture. Shape into small balls, the size is not important, except they should not be too large. Drop into boiling water and cook for about 5 minutes. Drain and serve in hot clear stock or consommé.

Depending on the size of the dumplings, serve 2 or 3 to each bowl of soup.

## SEMOLINA DUMPLINGS (*Griessnockerl*)    Austria

4–6 servings:
½oz (15g,1tb) butter or other fat
1 egg, well beaten
pinch of salt
4oz (125g,¾cup) coarse semolina

Cream the butter, beat in the egg, add a pinch of salt and the semolina. Mix thoroughly and leave covered for about half an hour. Have ready some boiling stock. Scoop out teaspoonfuls of the semolina mixture. Drop these into the stock. When all are in the pan, lower the heat and simmer for 15 to 20 minutes, or when the dumplings have risen to the top of the liquid.

## CHEESE DUMPLINGS (*Tvarohovčhé těsta*)    Czechoslovakia

4–6 servings:
8oz (250g,1cup) curd or cottage cheese
2 eggs, lightly beaten
2tb butter, melted
3oz (90g,½cup) fine semolina
½tsp salt

Rub the cheese through a sieve and mix with the remaining ingredients. Knead to a dough—it should be fairly stiff but if not, add more flour. Break off pieces, roll these into balls and cook in rapidly boiling water for 8 to 10 minutes. Test one to see if it is cooked through: if it is still raw inside, return it to the pan and cook a minute or so longer.

Serve sprinkled with melted butter, brown sugar, buttered bread-crumbs, or a fruit sauce.

## CROÛTON DUMPLINGS (*Housekové knedlíčky*)    Czechoslovakia

4–6 servings:
3–4 small stale bread rolls
butter, for frying
1 large egg
¾pt (3dl, 2cups) milk, fresh or sour
1lb (½kg, 4cups) plain flour
1tsp salt      1tsp baking powder

First prepare the croûtons. Cut the crust from the rolls. Cut out the soft portions into small cubes. Heat enough butter (or other fat) to cover the bottom of a thick frying pan. When it is smoking hot, add the cubed bread and fry until a golden brown. Take out and drain on kitchen paper. Leave until cool.

Beat the egg, add the milk and continue beating. Gradually add the flour, salt and baking powder and continue beating briskly until all the flour is mixed into the liquid. It should make a thick, firm batter which can hold its shape. Add the croûtons, put aside and 'rest' for 30 minutes.

Have ready a large pan with plenty of bubbling boiling water. Break off pieces of the dough with wet hands and form the pieces into dumplings. Drop into the boiling water, cover the pan and cook the dumplings for 20 to 30 minutes, depending on their size. Some cooks prefer to make walnut-sized dumplings and serve them whole, others make large ones which are cut with string into serving portions.

Serve with thick gravy, boiled meats, paprika dishes, etc. Also with hot melted butter and brown sugar.

## POTATO DUMPLING WITH SMOKED PORK (1)
### (*Špekové knedlíčky*)   Czechoslovakia

4–6 servings:
2lb (1kg) floury potatoes
salt to taste
2oz (60g,4tb) lard or butter
3 egg yolks
4oz (125g,1cup,heaped) fine breadcrumbs
¾lb (375g) smoked pork, diced
3 egg whites

Cook the potatoes in their skins in salted water until soft. Drain, cool and peel. Rub through a ricer into a mixing bowl. Soften the fat, add to the potatoes and beat until the fat is well blended in. Add the egg yolks one at a time, beating well after each addition. Add the breadcrumbs, mix well then add the pork. Beat the egg whites until stiff and fold into the potato mixture. Rinse a white napkin in hot water and squeeze it dry. Place the potato mixture in the centre, shape into a fat sausage and wrap in the cloth as for roly-poly pudding. Tie tightly at either end but lightly in the middle to allow room for some expansion. Put into a pan with boiling water and cook in constantly boiling water for 20 minutes.

To serve, take the dumpling from the pan, unwrap and place on a hot plate. Cut into thick slices. Czechs serve sauerkraut or a lettuce salad with this. Cold cooked pork or ham may be used instead of smoked pork.

Left-over dumpling can be sliced, dipped in beaten egg and breadcrumbs, fried in shallow fat and served with a sauce.


## POTATO DUMPLINGS WITH SMOKED PORK (2)
### (*Špekové knedlíčky*)   Czechoslovakia

6 servings:
1½lb (¾kg) floury potatoes
½lb (250g,1½ cups) fine semolina
salt to taste
1 egg

flour, for sprinkling
½lb (250g) smoked pork, diced
melted butter to garnish

Wash the potatoes and cook them in their skins in boiling salted water until soft. Cool, peel and mash. Make sure they are quite free from lumps. Add the semolina and a little salt and knead to a dough. Add the egg and continue kneading until the dough is pliable.

Lightly sprinkle a pastry board with flour. Add the dough and roll it out to about ¼ inch thick. Cut into 12 squares or rounds. In the centre of each piece place some of the diced pork. Bring the edges together and shape the dough into dumplings.

Have ready a large pan with plenty of lightly salted boiling water. When the water is bubbling, add the dumplings one at a time (use a perforated spoon to prevent splashing) and cook for about 10 minutes, or until the dumplings rise to the top of the pan. Take the dumplings carefully from the water with the same spoon and prick each one with a fork. This lets out the steam and makes the dumplings lighter.

Serve 2 dumplings per portion sprinkled with melted butter and accompanied by hot cabbage or a vegetable salad.

Instead of smoked pork, cracklings (see page 101) or diced fat bacon can be used.


## POTATO DUMPLINGS (*Bramborové knedlíčky*)   Czechoslovakia

6 servings:
2lb (1kg) old potatoes
salt to taste
3½oz (100g,½cup) semolina
3oz (90g,¾cup) flour
2 eggs, well beaten

Cook the potatoes in their skins in boiling salted water until soft. Strain off the hot water. Drain the potatoes in cold water and, as soon as cool enough to handle, peel and mash. Combine with the semolina and flour, salt and the eggs. Knead to a dough then divide into 6 dumplings.

Have ready a large pan with briskly boiling, lightly salted water. Add the dumplings, stirring them gently to avoid their sticking to the bottom. They will take about 5 minutes to cook but after this time take one from the pan to test whether it is done. If not, return it to the pan and cook them all for a further 3 minutes.

Serve with boiled ham or pork, or with fried onions. Or as a sweet dish with melted butter sprinkled generously with brown sugar and buttered breadcrumbs. Another favourite way of serving these dumplings is with a mixture of sugar and freshly ground poppy seeds.

## POTATO DUMPLINGS (*Buabaspitzle*)   South Germany

4–6 servings:
1½lb (¾kg) floury potatoes
salt, nutmeg to taste
2 eggs, well beaten
1oz (30g,¼cup) plain flour

Wash the potatoes and cook without peeling in boiling salted water until soft. Drain, cool, peel and rub through a sieve or ricer. Mix with the remaining ingredients to a smooth dough. With floured hands, break off pieces and roll into cigar-like shapes narrowing to a point at both ends. Cook in gently boiling water for 5 to 7 minutes or until the dumplings float on top of the water (when adding the dumplings to the pan, stir them gently with a wooden spoon to avoid sticking). When ready, take out with a perforated spoon, drain and serve with a dish of sauerkraut, or with roast meat with thick gravy or a sauce.

## SHAGGY DUMPLINGS (*Chlupaté knedlíčky*)   Czechoslovakia

4–6 servings:
1–1½lb (½–¾kg) old potatoes
2 eggs
1tsp salt
plain flour

Peel the potatoes, wash them well then grate on a medium coarse grater. Drop into cold water and leave for about 1 hour. Lift out with a perforated spoon so that all the starch remains in the water. Drain well in a sieve and squeeze any remaining water from them. Beat the eggs with the salt in a mixing bowl. Add the potatoes, mix well then gradually add enough flour to combine the potatoes to make a soft dough to be scooped out easily with a spoon.

Have ready a large pan with boiling, lightly salted water. Take out the potato dough by tablespoonfuls and drop into the boiling water. Cook until they rise to the top of the pan and begin to bob on the surface, plus 3 minutes.

Shaggy dumplings usually are served with finely chopped onion fried in fat, with cracklings (see page 101), and in some parts of Central Europe with apple purée.

## POTATO CAKES (*Škubánky*)  Czechoslovakia

4–6 servings:
2lb (1kg) floury potatoes
salt to taste
6oz (180g, 1½cups) flour, sieved
lard or shortening
ground poppy seeds, for sprinkling
sugar, butter, for sprinkling

On first reading, this recipe might seem somewhat stodgy but this is not so. However, it is important to follow the instructions carefully, simple though they are.

Peel the potatoes and coarsely chop. Cook in boiling salted water until soft. Drain off the water but retain it and leave the potatoes in the pan. Mash the potatoes in the pan without adding any other liquid or butter. Spread the mashed potato over the bottom of the pan, it should be about 3 inches thick, and make several holes in the potato with a spoon, reaching to the bottom of the pan. Fill these holes with flour and then return enough of the potato liquid to completely cover the potatoes. Cover with the lid and cook over the lowest possible heat for 30 minutes.

Drain off the excess liquid, if any, add salt to taste and beat the potatoes hard with a wooden spoon until the potato and flour are thoroughly mixed and the mixture is smooth.

Heat a little lard. Dip a large metal spoon into this and scoop out spoonfuls of the potato or *Škubánky* and drop like dumplings on to a hot plate. Sprinkle with ground poppy seeds, sugar and butter or, if a savoury preparation is preferred, with fried chopped onions, or grated cheese and melted butter.

This is a typical Czech recipe and for potato lovers well worth trying. Any left-over *Škubánky* can be made into fried potato cakes, or Hoe Cakes. Spread the cold *Škubánky* on to a slab, cut into rounds, dip these into beaten egg, then into fine breadcrumbs. Heat enough lard or dripping in a frying pan and fry the cakes until a golden brown.

## POTATO CAKES FROM RAW POTATOES (*Bramborák*)
### Czechoslovakia

4–6 servings:
1lb (½kg) old potatoes
1 egg, well beaten
2tb milk
1oz (30g,¼cup) flour
salt, pepper to taste
pinch of dried marjoram
1 small onion, peeled and finely chopped
2–3 garlic cloves, finely chopped
fat, for medium-deep frying

Wash, peel and grate the potatoes and put them into a bowl with plenty of cold water. Leave them for an hour then take from the water with a perforated spoon thus leaving the starch at the bottom of the bowl. Wipe the potatoes dry in a cloth. Combine the egg and milk, beat well then add the flour, salt, pepper, marjoram, onion and garlic. Mix these ingredients into the potatoes.

Heat a fair quantity of fat in a thick pan until smoking hot. Drop tablespoonfuls of the potato mixture into the hot fat, slightly flatten the potato heaps with a wooden spoon and fry quickly, first on one side then on the other until brown on both sides. Take from the fat, drain quickly on kitchen paper and serve with a green salad, sour cream, or with apple purée.

## CURD DUMPLINGS (*Túrosgombòc*)  Hungary

It seems almost unfair to the rest of Central Europe to ascribe this recipe to Hungary. Curd dumplings of all kinds are made throughout the region. However, I learned how to make them in Hungary and have always used this recipe.

4–6 servings:
1lb (½kg,2cups) curd or cottage cheese
3 egg yolks
1oz (30g,2tb) butter
2oz (60g,½cup) plain flour
1½oz (45g,3tb) sugar
3 egg whites
brown sugar and cinnamon (see method)

Rub the cheese through a fine sieve into a mixing bowl. Add the egg yolks one at a time beating well after each addition. Beat the butter until soft, beat into the cheese then add the flour and sugar. Beat the egg whites until stiff and gently fold these in with a metal spoon.

Have ready a large pan with plenty of lightly salted boiling water. Drop the mixture into the boiling water in tablespoons. Cook for 10 to 12 minutes. Although the dumplings come to the top of the pan after 5 minutes, they must be allowed to continue cooking a further 5 minutes.

While they are cooking, prepare a mixture of brown sugar flavoured with cinnamon with which to sprinkle over the dumplings when they come from the pan. Or, instead of the sugar mixture, soft fried breadcrumbs and melted butter can be sprinkled over the top of the dumplings.

The above recipe makes 10 medium-sized dumplings. They are feather-light, shaggy in shape and quite delicious. And, like a soufflé, they should be served as soon as they are ready.

### SALZBURGER DUMPLINGS (*Salzburger Nockerln*)   Austria

These baked dumplings are the culinary pride of Salzburg. The Salz-
burgers say those who do not like them have no taste, and they add that
Austrian women who cannot make them have no talent for being a
housewife or cook. These dumplings were first made or 'discovered' at the
beginning of the seventeenth century and by, or under, the instruction
of one, Agide Dietrich von Raitenau, Archbishop of Salzburg, who
loved power, pomp and puddings.

Salzburger dumplings are mainly made of air, eggs and the smallest
quantity of flour. If not correctly handled, they collapse. If the right
heat is not applied, or there is a trace of draught, they flop. However,
despite this solemn Austrian warning I do not consider they are any
more difficult to make than a soufflé, and those attempting them should
not be discouraged.

3 servings:

¾oz (20g,1½tb) unsalted butter

4 egg whites

3tb caster or fine sugar

1tsp vanilla sugar (see page 26)

3 egg yolks

¾oz (20g,3tb) flour

It is wise to butter a shallow baking dish before preparing the dumplings
so that there is no delay between the final mixing of the egg whites and
adding them to the pan. Make sure that the oven is hot *before* the dish is
placed in it.

Beat the egg whites until stiff, add the sugar and vanilla sugar and
continue beating to a stiff meringue consistency. Take out 3 tablespoons
of the beaten egg whites, beat this into the egg yolks then fold the
mixture into the beaten egg whites. Sift the flour over the top of the mixture and then carefully fold in. This quantity makes 3 dumplings. Scoop
out one third with a large metal spoon. Place carefully in the prepared
baking dish and add the rest in the same manner, the three portions close
together.

Put the pan in a hot oven (425°F: 220°C: Gas 7) and bake for 8 to 10
minutes. Take the dumplings from the oven, bring them to the table to

serve in the dish they were cooked in. Make sure there is no draught en route and that there is no great difference in temperature between kitchen and dining room.

FRUIT DUMPLINGS (*Švestkové knedlíčky*)   Czechoslovakia

4–6 servings:
1 egg
1oz (30g,2tb) melted butter
½gill (½dl,⅓cup) milk
½tsp salt
8oz (250g,2cups) plain flour
1lb (½kg) fresh fruit (see method)
melted butter and sugar to garnish

Beat the egg and mix with the butter and milk. Add the salt. Sift the flour on to a board or in a mixing bowl, make a hole in the middle, add the egg mixture and mix into the flour. Make a firm dough, add more flour if required, then knead the dough until smooth. Break off small pieces and roll these into rounds. On each round place fruit (peeled and quartered where required as with apples or pears, stoned for plums, damsons, cherries and prunes, stoned and halved for apricots and peaches). Wrap the dough round the fruit and make sure that the covering is well sealed.

Have ready a large pan with plenty of boiling water. Drop the dumplings into the water and cook them rapidly for 8 to 10 minutes or until they rise to the top of the pan. Do not over-cook. Take each one from the water as soon as ready, sprinkle with melted butter and put into a colander until the rest of the dumplings are ready. Place on a hot plate, sprinkle with more melted butter and sugar, brown is the best for dumplings. Also extremely good with dumplings are crumbled dry curd or cottage cheese, browned or buttered breadcrumbs, and ground poppy seeds.

## FRUIT DUMPLINGS WITH CURD CHEESE DOUGH (*Ovocné knedlíčky z tvarohového těsta*) Czechoslovakia

4–6 servings:
1lb (½kg,2cups) curd or cottage cheese
2oz (60g,4tb) butter, softened
2oz (60g,¼cup) sugar
½lb (250g,2cups) flour
2tb fine semolina
salt to taste
3 eggs
24 dried, or fresh, apricots
extra curd or cottage cheese for garnishing
4oz (125g,½cup) unsalted butter, melted
brown sugar, for sprinkling

If using dried apricots, these should first be soaked overnight then gently cooked until tender and well drained. Fresh apricots must be very ripe.

Rub the cottage cheese through a fine sieve, add the butter then the sugar and beat well. Sift 1 cup of flour into the cheese and beat until the mixture is smooth. Add the semolina, a good pinch of salt and again work the mixture until smooth. Beat the eggs until smooth and beat into the cheese mixture. Add the rest of the flour. Beat again and when the dough is smooth and firm, roll it into a large sausage. Cut into slices and roll out each slice large enough to hold 1 apricot. Place an apricot on each piece of dough, fold it up so that the apricot is entirely wrapped in dough. Smooth into round dumplings.

Have ready a large pan with boiling, lightly salted water, add the dumplings and cook them for 15 to 20 minutes.

As soon as the dumplings are taken from the pan, punch a hole in each to allow the steam to escape. Serve immediately with crumbled curd or cottage cheese, melted butter and brown sugar. Some people also add powdered sugar; many families place a bowl of melted unsalted butter on the table for everyone to help himself.

These dumplings are extremely good but, when serving them, it is better to have only soup as a main course, then follow with a good helping of dumplings.

## NOODLES (*Spätzle*)   South Germany

This, according to the Swabians, is Germany's national dish, a point often disputed but certainly it is a national dish of South Germany. It is said that the Swabians are a progressive people but when it comes to making *Spätzle* they are downright conservative, especially the men, who argue that their precious *Spätzle* must be prepared as their great-grandmothers made them. The dough should be scraped from a wooden board with a special scraper or a knife and the *Spätzle* dropped into boiling water. Both knife and board require constant wetting in order that the mixture does not stick. The Swabian males regard the use of the modern *Spätzle* sieves almost with horror, housewives less so since they are the ones who make the *Spätzle*.

4–6 servings:

1lb (½kg, 4cups) plain flour

4 eggs

1tsp salt

4–5tb water

Sift the flour into a bowl, add the eggs and salt and beat well. Add half the water, again beat the dough then add enough of the remaining water to make a firm dough. Beat this long and hard until it positively bursts into bubbles. This can be done in an electric mixer, provided a Swabian male is not around. Put about one-third of the dough on to a wooden board, cut into strips and, with a spatula or knife, scrape the strips of dough into a large pan of rapidly boiling water. The board and knife should be repeatedly dipped into cold water. Repeat this operation with the rest of the dough, or push the dough through a sieve (see below). When the *Spätzle* rise to the top of the boiling water, take them out with a perforated spoon and drop at once into cold water. This dissolves the starch and they will not stick together. Take from the cold water, drain in a colander and at once put into a warm pan, add some hot butter and warm them over a low heat. Serve at once.

*Spätzle* usually are served with stews, goulash dishes, with game and sometimes with a cream sauce.

The *Spätzle* sieve is oblong with holes in it and fits across a large saucepan. It has a moveable combined cutter and pusher and the dough drops easily and quickly into the pan. I have no doubt that if great-grandmother had had a similar gadget she would have used it.

*Spätzle* also are prepared commercially.

### EGG-BARLEY (*Tarhonya*)   Hungary

This is a type of exceedingly stiff dough which is spread out to dry then grated on a coarse grater to form small barley-shaped pellets. These are then spread out again in the sun to dry or placed in an almost cool oven when there is no sun.

*Tarhonya* probably is one of the oldest of the dried foods and was used by the nomadic Magyar tribes on their long journeys. Even more recently, agricultural workers and shepherds in the Puszta carried *Tarhonya* with them so they could quickly prepare a meal over a twig fire.

*Tarhonya* is sold in a great many stores dealing with continental foods. To Cook *Tarhonya*:

4–6 servings:
2oz (60g,4tb) lard
½lb (250g) tarhonya
½tsp paprika pepper
salt to taste
1½oz (45g,3tb) melted butter

Heat the lard in a small pan, add the *Tarhonya* and fry until it is a golden brown. Sprinkle with paprika pepper, add water to cover and cook gently for 30 to 40 minutes or until all the liquid has evaporated. Add salt and the butter, shaking the pan from time to time to prevent sticking. Continue cooking gently, stirring frequently, until the *Tarhonya* is dark brown.

Serve as a garnish with any type of Hungarian goulash and thick soup.

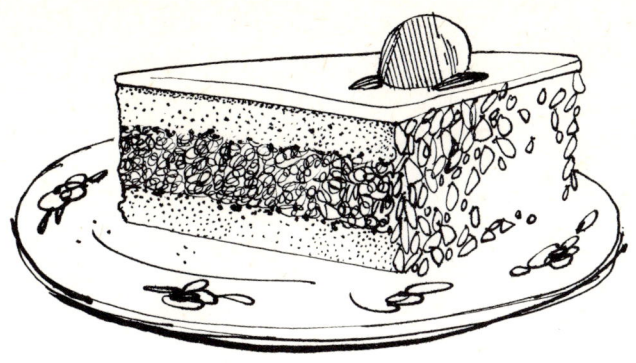

# CAKES and PUDDINGS

### SACHER CAKE (*Sacher Torte*)   Austria

This is Vienna's most famous cake, elegantly simple and for which there are many recipes, all 'authentic', 'original' and 'the one-and-only'. It was invented in 1832 by Franz Sacher, then Metternich's chef, who was asked by his employer for 'something new'. He could not have known what a success he was producing as he is reported to have said: 'I just flung together some ingredients, and there you are.'

The cake is a rich chocolate sponge sliced in half, spread with apricot jam, the pieces sandwiched together again and given a chocolate icing. Or the jam is spread over the top and the icing over this.

4–6 servings:
butter, for greasing
5oz (150g, 10tb) butter
8oz (250g, 1cup) sugar
8oz (250g, 8squares) bitter (baker's) chocolate
5 eggs
1tsp vanilla flavouring
4oz (125g, 1cup) cake or self-raising flour
apricot jam, for spreading
chocolate icing or frosting (see method)

Rub a 9-inch cake pan with butter.

Beat the butter until soft then gradually add 4 tablespoons of the sugar and continue beating until the mixture is creamy. Melt half the chocolate in the top of a double boiler. While it is still hot, add it to the creamed butter and beat well. Separate the eggs. Add the yolks one by one, beating vigorously after each addition. Continue to beat until the mixture is light and frothy. Beat the egg whites until stiff, add 4 tablespoons of sugar and the vanilla. Continue beating until a meringue consistency is reached—the mixture will stand in stiff peaks. Fold the egg whites into the cake batter. Sift the flour twice and then fold it into the cake mixture. Pour into a 9in buttered cake pan and bake in a moderate oven (350°F: 180°C: Gas 4) for about 1 hour. Take the cake from the oven, turn it out from the pan and leave it to become quite cold. Warm the jam and spread it over the cake. Cover top and sides with chocolate icing. Place the cake on a round plate and cut before serving.

Chocolate Icing (Frosting):

Break the remaining chocolate into small pieces and melt in the top of a double boiler over hot water. Dissolve the remaining sugar in 2 tablespoons warm water and then cook in a small pan to the thread stage (to test: cool a little, dip in index finger, press against thumb, and a thread should form when finger and thumb are separated), or until just beginning to thicken. Take from the pan and cool. Stir the melted chocolate, add the cooled sugar syrup and continue stirring until the mixture thickens. Spread this over the cake over the top and round the sides. It is important that the thickness of the jam and the icing should be the same.

It has become fashionable to serve whipped cream with *Sacher torte* in Vienna. This is not traditional but extremely good. However, it is not served unless asked for.

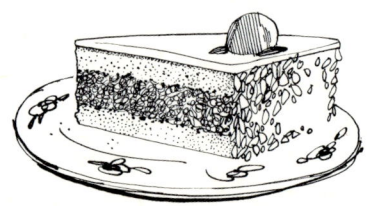

## CHOCOLATE LAYER CAKE (*Csokoládètorta*) Hungary

4–6 servings:
butter, for greasing pan
3oz (90g, 6tb) unsalted butter
3oz (90g, ⅔cup) caster or fine sugar
6 eggs
3oz (90g, ½cup) unpeeled almonds, finely ground
5oz (150g, 5 squares) bitter chocolate, grated
2oz (60g, ¾cup) breadcrumbs, finely sifted
½tsp grated lemon rind

Brush two 9-inch cake pans generously with butter.

Beat the butter until soft, add the sugar and beat until creamy. Separate the eggs and add the egg yolks one at a time, beating thoroughly after each addition. Add the almonds, grated chocolate, breadcrumbs and lemon rind and beat. If beating by hand, the complete beating should take 20 minutes; in an electric blender this can be achieved in 5 to 7 minutes. Beat the egg whites until stiff. Fold these into the chocolate cake mixture. Pour the mixture into the prepared cake pans and bake for about 45 minutes in a moderate oven (350°F: 180°C: Gas 4). Before taking from the oven, test with a knife. If it comes out clean they are ready.

Leave the cakes until quite cold, then cut each horizontally into two rounds, thus making four rounds of cake. Three rounds can be spread with a chocolate cream (see below) or with slightly warmed apricot jam. Place the layers, one on top of the other using whichever filling is preferred. The top can be sprinkled lightly with sifted icing (confectioner's) sugar or with icing (see Sacher Cake) if preferred.

Chocolate Cream Filling:
4oz (125g, 4 squares) melted bitter (baker's) chocolate
6oz (180g, ⅔cup) unsalted butter
2 egg yolks
2oz (60g, ¼cup) caster or fine sugar

Melt the chocolate in the top of a double boiler over boiling water. Beat the butter until soft, add the egg yolks one at a time and continue beating until the mixture is light and fluffy. Add the sugar and finally the melted chocolate.

This cake is rich and can be served as a sweet dish after a meal. Sometimes whipped cream is served with it.

## CURD CHEESE CAKE (*Tvarohový koláč*)   Czechoslovakia

4–6 servings:
4oz (125g,scant cup) shelled hazelnuts or walnuts
butter, for greasing
3oz (90g,scant cup) fine breadcrumbs
4oz (125g,½cup) butter
4oz (125g,½cup) fine sugar
4 eggs
4oz (125g,½cup) curd or cottage cheese
warmed jam, grated chocolate and finely chopped nuts, to garnish

Put the nuts into a thick but dry pan and quickly toast over a good heat until they begin to brown. Stir all the time or they will burn. Coarsely crush.

Rub an 8-inch round cake pan (or the equivalent size loaf pan) generously with butter and sprinkle with some of the breadcrumbs. Cream the measured butter with the sugar. Separate the eggs. Add the egg yolks one at a time, beating well after each addition. Rub the cheese through a sieve, add the creamed butter mixture. Beat the egg whites until stiff and fold into the curd cheese dough using a metal spoon, adding fine breadcrumbs alternately. Add the nuts. Pile into the prepared cake pan and bake in a moderate oven (350°F: 180°C: Gas 4) for 45 minutes or until the top feels firm and a knife inserted into it comes out clean. Take from the oven and let the cake cool in the pan. Carefully turn out.

When ready to use, spread lightly with jam and sprinkle generously with grated chocolate and chopped nuts.

This cake can be served as a sweet dish after a meal or as a cake at tea-time. It bears no resemblance to the conventional cheese cake.

## HAZELNUT CAKE (*Linzer Torte*)  Austria

There are several versions of this popular cake. This one is for what is called brown *Linzer Torte*. The original cake came from Linz but curiously enough it is thought that the original does not match up to the so-called copies.

4–6 servings:
4½oz (140g,9tb) butter
4½oz (140g,scant1¼cups) flour
4½oz (140g,1cup) shelled hazelnuts
4½oz (140g,full½cup) sugar
cinnamon, ground cloves to taste
1tsp grated lemon rind
1 egg
1 hard egg yolk
redcurrant jam to garnish    extra egg to glaze
caster, icing or confectioner's sugar for sprinkling

Rub the butter into the flour until it is like fine breadcrumbs. Grind the nuts. Add these to the butter and flour, then add sugar, cinnamon and ground cloves, lemon rind, the whole egg and the hard egg yolk. Mix this to a dough. Put two-thirds of this at the bottom of a shallow spring-form cake pan, pushing it down gently with your fingers. Spread it with jam. Roll out the rest of the dough and cut into finger-thick strips. Arrange these over the top of the cake in a lattice work pattern. Keep one long piece to go round the outside edge of the cake to make it look neat. Beat the remaining egg with 1 tablespoon of water and brush it over the top of the cake.

Bake in a moderately hot oven (350°F: 180°C: Gas 4) until it is brown, about 45 minutes. Take from the pan, let it become cold then sprinkle with powdered sugar.

Here is an unusual version of the *Linzer Torte*. Divide your pastry into two rounds the size of your cake pan. Put one layer on the bottom of the pan, on top place layers of *oblaten* wafers (see page 172) each spread with jam, leaving an edge of about 1 inch all round. Brush this with beaten egg. Cut the remaining pastry into strips and arrange lattice fashion and continue as above.

## HONEY CAKE (*Perník*) Czechoslovakia

There are many recipes for *perník* but this is one of the more simple ones.

4–6 servings:
5oz (150g, ⅔cup) sugar
½oz (15g, 1tb) baking powder
1lb (½kg, 4cups) flour
¼tsp each ground cinnamon, ground cloves, ground allspice, caraway seeds
¼tsp vanilla flavouring
½lb (250g, ¾cup) liquid honey
2oz (60g, 4tb) butter
¼pt (1dl, ⅔cup) black coffee
1 large egg, well beaten
butter, for greasing

Sieve the sugar, baking powder, flour and spices into a warm mixing bowl. Mix thoroughly. Warm the honey in a small pan, add the butter and stir until it is dissolved into the honey. Beat the coffee into the egg. Add the vanilla. Combine the honey and egg and beat well then pour this mixture into the flour mixture. Work it to a dough. Cover and leave for 2 hours. If the dough should become too stiff (and it might if the kitchen is not warm), put it into a warm place to soften.

Rub a loaf-shaped baking pan with butter and sprinkle lightly with flour. Pour the honey dough into the pan and brush the top with black coffee. Put into a hot oven (425°F: 220°C: Gas 7) and leave for 5 minutes. Reduce the heat to moderately hot (350°F: 180°C: Gas 4) and continue cooking for 40 to 45 minutes.

If the *perník* is baked too quickly, a crust forms on the top but the inside remains soft and gooey. If the oven is too slow, then the cake becomes too dry. The ideal is a soft, slightly tacky texture. Let the *perník* cool in the pan in which it is baked. Take from the pan, put into an airtight container and keep for a week before cutting.

Although called a cake, *perník* is much more like a sweet bread. It is particularly good cut into fairly thick slices and generously spread with unsalted butter, or served with soft, fresh curd or cottage cheese. The black coffee called for in the recipe should be fresh, real coffee, not instant.

## POPPY SEED CAKE (*Makový koláč*)  Czechoslovakia

4–6 servings:
butter, for greasing
breadcrumbs, for sprinkling
2oz (60g,4tb) unsalted butter
8oz (250g,1cup) caster or fine sugar
6 egg yolks
2oz (60g,½cup) sultanas (white raisins)
½lb (250g,1½cups) poppy seeds
lemon juice and rind of 1 lemon
½tsp ground cinnamon
¼tsp ground cloves
6 egg whites
jam, for spreading

Before starting on the cake, either grind the poppy seeds in a liquidiser or pound in a mortar with a pestle. Rub two 9-inch layer cake pans generously with butter and sprinkle lightly with breadcrumbs.

Cream the measured butter with the sugar. Beat the egg yolks until thick and fluffy. Beat into the creamed butter. Add the sultanas, poppy seeds, lemon juice and rind and spices. Mix thoroughly. Beat the egg whites until stiff. Fold into the batter.

Pour the batter into the prepared cake pans and bake in a moderate oven (350°F: 180°C: Gas 4) for about 30 minutes or until the cake is firm to the touch. Cool the layers in the pans. Turn out, spread one layer with jam (apricot, strawberry or raspberry) and cover with the remaining layer of cake.

Serve topped with stiffly whipped cream or spread with a rum-flavoured glacé icing (frosting).

## PLUM CAKE OR TART (*Zwetschenkuchen*)  Austria

4–6 servings:
For pastry:
14oz (400g,3½cups) flour
6oz (180g,⅔cup) unsalted butter
3oz (90g,⅓cup) sugar
pinch of salt
2 egg yolks
½tsp lemon rind, grated
For filling:
1½lb (¾kg) ripe damsons or plums
For sponge:
4 eggs
2oz (60g,½cup) flour
3oz (90g,⅓cup) sugar
caster or fine sugar, for dusting

First prepare a sweet short pastry. Heap the flour on to a pastry board or in a bowl if this is preferred, the only essential is that the board or bowl is cool. Make a hole in the centre of the flour, add the butter (it is best cut into slivers), sugar, salt, egg yolks and lemon rind. Work these ingredients together with the fingertips, a sticky business it is true, then gradually gather in the flour. Add 2 to 3 tablespoons of cold water to make the dough pliable but be careful not to add too much, the pastry must be short. Work the dough to a ball then knead until it is very smooth and pliable. Let the dough rest at least 30 minutes, preferably longer, overnight if this is convenient. This quantity of pastry should be sufficient to completely cover the average baking or cookie sheet.

Wash the plums, cut each into half and remove the stone. Cut each half into two. Put aside.

Roll out the pastry about ¼ inch thick to fit the baking sheet. Heat the oven to moderate (350°F: 180°C: Gas 4), add the pastry and bake 'blind' until it just begins to change colour and is set.

While it is cooking, make the sponge mixture. Beat the eggs. Sieve the flour into a bowl, add the eggs and beat until smooth then add the sugar.

Take the pastry from the oven. Arrange the plums on top in neat rows each just touching the other, cut side uppermost. Spread the sponge mixture over the top, return the cake to the oven and continue baking until the sponge is a pale golden colour and a knife inserted in it comes out clean. Serve cold dusted with fine sugar.

Instead of plums, sliced apples, halved or quartered apricots, small quartered peaches, ripe stoned cherries, or very ripe pears may be used.

## POTATO SPONGE CAKE (*Burgonyatorta*)    Hungary

This recipe produces a light, almost nutty sponge cake with no suggestion of potatoes and it never seems to flop as some sponge cakes do. If ground almonds are not available, it can be made with finely ground sweet biscuit (cookie) crumbs. For the filling, use a whole fruit jam, ideally apricot.

4–6 servings:
butter, for greasing
½lb (¼kg) floury potatoes, well cooked
2oz (60g,⅓cup) ground sweet almonds
3oz (90g,⅓cup) fine sugar
1tsp lemon rind, grated
2 whole eggs
4 egg yolks
4 egg whites
icing (confectioner's) sugar for sprinkling

Rub a 9 to 10 inch-deep cake pan generously with butter. Push the potatoes through a ricer or mash with a potato masher until smooth. Combine with the almonds, sugar, lemon rind, the 2 whole eggs and the 4 egg yolks. Mix well and beat for 20 minutes by hand or 5 minutes in an electric blender. Beat the egg whites until stiff. Fold into the potato batter. Pour this mixture into the prepared cake pan and bake in a very moderate oven (325°F: 160°C: Gas 3) until a golden brown. Take from the oven, turn out on a cake rack to cool.

When the cake is quite cold cut into three layers. Spread one layer with jam, cover with a second layer, spread this with jam and cover with the third layer. Sprinkle the top with icing (confectioner's) sugar and serve.

STUDENTS' BREAD (*Diàkpudding*)   Hungary

4–6 servings:
4oz (125g,1cup) shelled walnuts
4oz (125g,1cup) blanched almonds
4oz (125g,1cup) shelled hazelnuts
4oz (125g,1cup) stoned dates
4oz (125g,⅔cup) raisins
4oz (125g,1cup) figs
4oz (125g,1cup) candied orange peel
4oz (125g,1cup) stoned dried prunes
4–5 whole eggs
8oz (250g,1cup) icing or confectioner's sugar
2–3tb rum or brandy
1lb (500g,4cups) flour
butter, for greasing

Put the first 8 ingredients through the coarse blade of a mincing machine, or chop everything very finely. Beat the eggs with the sugar until thick, add the rum and beat this mixture into the minced fruit and nuts and blend thoroughly. Add the flour and work the mixture until smooth. Rub a large loaf pan with butter and sprinkle with flour. Add the fruit mixture and bake in a moderate oven (350°F: 180°C: Gas 4) until brown or when a knife comes out clean after insertion.

Instead of rum or brandy, lemon juice may be used; also grated lemon rind, powdered cloves and ground cinnamon may be added.

BISHOP'S BREAD (*Bischofsbrot*)   Austria

This is a fruit cake, not a bread, and there are many different recipes agreeing only in the shape of the cake pan in which it is baked, a shallow oblong pan with a rounded bottom deeply indented along its length and ribbed to give the bread its characteristic shape. However, the cake can be baked equally well in any shallow oblong pan. Do not fill the pan more than three-quarters full.

4–6 servings:
butter, for greasing
extra flour, for dusting
4 eggs
4oz (125g,1cup) self-raising or cake flour
1tsp lemon rind, grated
2oz (60g,⅓cup) glacé cherries
2oz (60g,2squares) bitter (baker's) chocolate
4oz (125g,½cup) caster or fine sugar
2oz (60g,⅓cup) seedless raisins
2oz (60g,⅓cup) nuts, finely chopped
Either hazelnuts or almonds can be used for this cake.

Rub the cake pan with butter and lightly dust with flour. Separate the egg yolks from the whites. Sift the flour into a mixing bowl. Add the lemon rind. Chop the cherries and grate the chocolate. Beat the egg yolks until smooth, add half the sugar and continue beating until the mixture is frothy. Whisk the egg whites until stiff, add the rest of the sugar and continue beating until the mixture forms peaks as for meringues. Fold in the egg yolks then the flour, folding it in carefully with a metal spoon. Add the chocolate, cherries, raisins and finally the nuts. Pour the mixture into the prepared pan and bake in a moderate oven (350°F: 180°C: Gas 4) for 45 minutes but check after 30 minutes. Take from the oven, leave until cool and then gently turn out on to a wire rack. Leave for one day before eating.

ALMOND BOWS (*Mandel Bretzeln*)   South Germany

4–6 servings:
4oz (125g,½cup) unsalted butter
3 large eggs
8oz (250g,2cups) plain flour
8oz (250g,1½cups) ground almonds

Beat the butter in a warmed mixing bowl until creamy. Add 2 eggs, one at a time, beating well after each addition. Add the flour and, when thoroughly mixed, add the almonds. Mix well and gently knead to a smooth dough. Roll this out on a lightly floured board to $\frac{1}{8}$ inch thick. Cut into strips of 6 inches long. Tie into bows. Beat the remaining egg. Lightly grease a baking sheet, arrange the bows on this—they should not touch—brush with beaten egg and bake in a moderate oven (350°F: 180°C: Gas 4) for 8 to 10 minutes or until they are a golden brown.

### GOD'S FAVOURS (*Boží Milosti*)    Czechoslovakia

4–6 servings:
2 egg yolks, lightly beaten
2tb cream
2tb rum or brandy
10oz (300g, 2½cups) plain flour
½tsp baking powder
¼tsp salt
oil, for deep frying
icing (confectioner's) sugar, for sprinkling

Beat the egg yolks into the cream, add the rum, mix well, add the flour, baking powder and salt. Mix to a firm dough (a little more flour may be required, it depends on its quality). Knead the dough on a floured board until smooth. Roll out to $\frac{1}{8}$ inch thick. Cut into squares or diamond shapes 3in x 3in and in the centre of each piece, cut two inch-long slits. Heat the oil until very hot, add the pieces of dough 2 or 3 at a time, depending on the size of the pan and fry until the pieces have swollen and are a golden brown on both sides, a matter of a few seconds. Take from the pan, quickly drain on absorbent paper and, while still hot, sprinkle lightly with icing (confectioner's) sugar.

A little sugar, also grated lemon or orange rind may be added to the dough while mixing.

### CHERRY SQUARES (*Bublanina*)   Czechoslovakia

This cake also is translated as Bubble Cake. Although stoned fresh cherries are usually used in its preparation, other fruit may be used instead.

4–6 servings:

1–1½lb (½–¾kg) ripe sweet cherries

butter, for greasing

4oz (125g,½cup) unsalted butter

4oz (125g,½cup) sugar

3 egg yolks

4oz (125g,1cup) self-raising or cake flour

¼tsp salt

1tsp baking powder

3–4tb milk

1tsp lemon rind, grated

3 egg whites

vanilla sugar (see page 26) to taste

Wash and stone the cherries and make sure they are quite dry before adding them to the cake mixture. If they are wet, they will make the sponge soggy. Rub a 10-inch square baking pan generously with butter.

Warm the unsalted butter slightly until it begins to soften and beat it with the sugar until creamy. Add the egg yolks one at a time, beating well after each addition. Sieve the flour with the salt and baking powder. Gradually add this to the creamed butter alternately with the milk. Add the lemon rind and beat until the mixture is light and fluffy. Beat the egg whites until stiff and fold these into the batter.

Pour the batter into the prepared baking tin, it should be about 1 inch thick, and arrange the cherries on the top to completely cover the batter.

Bake in a moderate oven (350°F: 180°C: Gas 4) until the top is a golden brown, 35 to 40 minutes.

Sprinkle lightly with vanilla sugar before serving and cut into squares.

### NUREMBERG GINGER NUTS (*Nürnberger Braune Lebkuchen*)

4–6 servings:
¾lb (375g,1cup) honey
6oz (180g,¾cup) sugar
1½lb (¾kg,6cups) plain flour
1tsp baking powder
pinch of baking soda
½gill (¼dl,⅓cup) water
½lb (250g,1cup) almonds, chopped
½tsp each ground cloves, cinnamon, ginger
3oz (90g,scant cup) candied orange peel, chopped
3oz (90g,scant cup) candied lemon peel, chopped

Bring the honey with half the sugar to boiling point and keep boiling until the liquid drops in beads from a spoon. Leave to cool. Sift the flour into a mixing bowl, add the cooled honey, the baking powder and soda. Mix well, knead into a smooth dough and leave for 2 days.

Boil the remaining sugar with the water to a syrup. Add the almonds and quickly brown them. Blend the syrup and almonds into the dough as swiftly as possible, adding the spices. Roll out the dough on to a floured board. Cut into squares or ovals with a sharp knife. Finely chop the peel, sprinkle this over the ginger nuts and leave in a warm place until the next day.

Bake in a warm oven (325°F: 160°C: Gas 3) until brown and, while still warm, brush with a sugar glaze or leave until cold and lightly spread with glacé icing (frosting).

### SHORTBREAD BISCUITS (Cookies) (*Pogàcsa*)   Hungary

25–30 biscuits
8oz (250g,2cups) plain flour
pinch of salt
6oz (180g,¾cup) butter
1 large egg      1 egg yolk
25–30 whole almonds, salted

Sift the flour and salt into a mixing bowl. Rub in the butter until the mixture looks like coarse breadcrumbs. Add the whole egg and mix to a firm dough. Roll out to about ½ inch thick. Cut into small rounds or other shapes. Beat the egg yolk and brush the tops of the biscuits. Put 1 salted almond on top of each shortbread. Leave for 30 minutes. Heat the oven to moderate (350°F: 180°C: Gas 4), add the biscuits and bake until they are a pale golden colour.

Serve cold with wine.

## ZWIEBACK (*Lomnický suchar*)   Czechoslovakia

From several recipes for zwieback I have chosen the simplest. Some add a little sugar, also freshly grated lemon peel and nutmeg, also a little fennel. The zwieback can be kept for quite a while in an airtight container.

30–35 zwieback

¾oz (25g,1cake) dried yeast

1lb (½kg,4cups) plain flour

1tsp salt

4oz (125g,½cup) butter

3 egg yolks, lightly beaten

scant ½pt (¼l,1cup) milk

Put the yeast into a small bowl, add a little warm water and leave until the yeast rises. A little sugar can be added to assist this process.

Sieve the flour and salt into a mixing bowl. Cut in the butter and mix in thoroughly. Combine the egg yolks with the milk and yeast. Pour into the flour, stir and mix to a smooth dough. If necessary add a little more flour since the quality of flour and the size of eggs varies considerably. Knead the dough until quite smooth and pliable, then put into a dry warm bowl, cover and leave until it doubles its bulk. Break into 2 or 3 pieces and shape into long sausages or like French loaves. Put these on a greased baking or cookie sheet, again cover and leave until the dough has again risen. Bake in a moderate oven (350°F: 180°C: Gas 4) until the loaves are a golden brown. Take from the oven, ease off the baking sheet and leave until the following day. Cut into slices and bake in a fairly hot oven (400°F: 200°C: Gas 6) until dry. While the slices are still hot from this final baking, sprinkle them either with vanilla or icing (confectioner's) sugar.

## MALAKOFF CAKE (*Malakofftorte*)    Austria

This cake, although heavy on cream, has the advantage that it requires no cooking. It is made in a spring-form cake pan and served with stiffly whipped cream, ice-cold. Sponge fingers are also called Savoy biscuits.

6–8 servings:

30–40 sponge fingers

4oz (125g,½cup) unsalted butter

4oz (125g,½cup) sugar

3 egg yolks

4oz (125g,⅔cup) ground almonds

2pts (1l,5cups) double or thick cream

rum or brandy to taste

First prepare the filling. Beat the butter until soft, add the sugar and continue beating until the mixture is creamy. Add the egg yolks, beating vigorously after each addition, then add the almonds and a quarter of the cream. Beat the rest of the cream until stiff.

Split the sponge fingers across into halves. Arrange a layer on the bottom of a cake pan. Sprinkle with rum to taste. Spread with the butter cream then with a layer of whipped cream. Add another layer of the sponge fingers, butter cream and whipped cream and continue in the manner until all the ingredients are used up, the top layer being of sponge fingers. Press them down, cover and place on ice or in the refrigerator for 6 hours. Take the cake from the pan and serve with whipped cream.

## APPLE PIE (*Jablkový koláč*)  Czechoslovakia

4–6 servings:
butter, for greasing
fine breadcrumbs, for sprinkling
2oz (60g,¼cup) sugar
3oz (90g,6tb) butter
6oz (180g,1½cups) plain flour
1tsp lemon rind, grated
1 egg yolk, lightly beaten
2tsp baking powder
1tb milk
1–1½lb (½–¾kg) cooking apples
brown sugar to taste
ground cinnamon to taste
walnuts, grated, to taste

Rub a shallow pie-plate with butter and lightly sprinkle with bread-crumbs. Rub the measured quantity of sugar into the butter, add the flour, lemon rind, egg yolk, baking powder and milk and mix to a dough. Divide into 2 pieces and roll each piece out to a round to fit the pie-plate. Put aside.

Peel and thickly slice the apples. Stew these for a few minutes in a little water, enough to just soften them. Drain. Put one round of the pastry over the prepared pie-plate, spread with the cooked apples, sprinkle with brown sugar, cinnamon and walnuts. Cover with the remaining pastry. Puncture small holes with a fork on the top of the pie to let out the steam. Make small rosettes with any scraps of left-over pastry around the holes. Bake in a moderately hot oven (350°F: 180°C: Gas 4) for 20 to 30 minutes or until the top is a light golden colour.

If the apples are soft (quick cookers), it is not necessary to stew them before adding to the pie-plate.

I once served Czech guests with my own English version of apple pie to be thanked almost with tears in their eyes for serving 'one of our national dishes'. The only difference I can see is that the British seldom sweeten their pastry.

### APPLE SPONGE (*Jablkový koláč*)   Czechoslovakia

4–6 servings:
1lb (½kg) cooking apples
butter, for greasing
3oz (90g,6tb) butter
6oz (180g,¾cup) sugar
4 egg yolks
6oz (180g,1½cups) plain flour
2oz (60g,½cup) cornflour (cornstarch)
1tsp baking powder
4tb (5tb) milk
4 egg whites
vanilla sugar (see page 26), for sprinkling
1oz (30g,2tb) melted butter

Peel the apples, slice fairly thinly and leave in cold water to prevent them going brown. Rub a 9-inch square baking pan generously with butter.

Beat the butter and sugar until creamy, add the egg yolks one at a time, beating well until the mixture is light and fluffy. Sieve the flour with the cornflour and baking powder. Gradually add this to the creamed butter alternately with the milk. Beat the mixture until very creamy. Beat the egg whites until stiff and fold with a metal spoon into the batter. Pour the batter into the prepared baking tin. Pat the apples dry and arrange in parallel rows neatly over the top, sprinkle with vanilla sugar and melted butter and bake in a moderate oven (350°F: 180°C: Gas 4) for 30 to 45 minutes or until the sponge has risen and is a golden brown on top.

### 'SPONGY' OMELETTE VIENNA STYLE (*Wiener Biskuit-Omelette*)
Austria

1 serving:
1tb plain flour
pinch of salt
2 eggs
½oz (15g,1tb) butter

Sieve the flour into a bowl, add the salt and separate the eggs. Add the egg yolks and beat well until the mixture is smooth. Beat the egg whites until stiff. Heat the butter in a thick frying pan (preferably one reserved only for omelettes). Fold the egg whites into the egg batter and pour it all into the hot pan. With a palette knife lift the batter round the edges to prevent sticking and cook over a moderate heat until the underneath is a light brown. Put the pan under a grill and let the top rise and cook to a golden brown.

The omelette can be eaten plain but more generally is served with jam or fruit preserve.

## DRUNKEN CAPUCHIN (*Besoffener Kapuziner*)   Austria

4 servings:
4 egg yolks
2oz (60g,¼cup) white sugar
2oz (60g,2squares) bitter (baker's) chocolate, finely grated
ground cloves, cinnamon to taste
1tsp grated lemon rind
4 egg whites
1oz (30g,2tb) white sugar
3oz (90g,1scant cup) fine breadcrumbs
butter, for greasing
extra breadcrumbs, for sprinkling
2 cups (2½cups) mulled wine (see method)
powdered sugar to taste

Combine the egg yolks with the first quantity of sugar and beat until the mixture is thick and frothy. Add the chocolate, cloves, cinnamon and lemon rind. Beat the egg whites until stiff, add the remaining white sugar and continue beating until the mixture stands in peaks. Fold in the breadcrumbs and the egg yolk mixture. Rub 4 small baking dishes with butter, sprinkle with fine breadcrumbs and three-quarters fill with the cake mixture. Bake in a moderate oven (350°F: 180°C: Gas 4) for 25 to 30 minutes or until the mixture feels firm but still soft when a finger is lightly passed over the top.

To serve, turn out and generously pour the mulled wine over the top plus the powdered sugar. Can be served hot or cold.

Mulled Wine (*Glühwein*):
1 bottle red table wine
¼pt (1dl,⅔cup) water
½lb (¼kg) sugar
2 cloves
1 inch cinnamon stick
lemon peel to taste

Boil all the ingredients, except the wine, and reduce the quantity by half. Strain, return to the pot, add the wine and bring almost to boiling point.

## CHESTNUT CREAM (*Gesztenyepürè*)   Hungary

When my husband and I lived in Hungary in the late 'thirties we stayed for several months in a hotel on one of Budapest's main streets. On the pavement opposite was a fruit stall run by a hard-working man-and-wife team, the husband a Jew. I remember them best for their delicious peaches and apricots—and their creamed chestnuts. These they prepared themselves and sold in the winter months. We became friends and I was a regular customer for their chestnuts which we gorged with whipped cream. One day they asked us to have a meal with them in their small flat. How we ate. Today I never eat creamed chestnuts without thinking of this genial couple, of their simple hospitality, of their lovely fruits, and I wonder, with sadness, what happened to them.

4–6 servings:
2lb (1kg) chestnuts
milk to cover
½lb (250g,1cup) sugar  ·
½pt (¼l,1¼cups) water
vanilla flavouring to taste
1pt (½l,2½cups) double or thick cream

Cook the chestnuts in boiling water until they can easily be peeled, both the inner and outer skins. The time for this operation varies according to the chestnuts, from 10 to possibly 30 minutes. Cool, remove both skins and return the shelled chestnuts to the pan, cover with milk and cook gently until the chestnuts are very soft. Rub through a sieve or, better still, through a ricer, when they will come out like little grains of rice.

While the chestnuts are cooking, cook the sugar in another pan with the water to make a thick syrup but do not let it become brown. Mix this with the chestnuts (after they have been sieved or riced), add a little vanilla flavouring and cool. Whip the cream until stiff. Mix half the cream into the chestnuts and pile pyramid shape on a plate. Add the rest of the cream, letting it fall from the top of the pyramid down the sides.

Chill before serving.

## PANCAKES (*Palacsinta*)   Hungary

This recipe will produce 10 to 12 thin, medium-sized pancakes. Use a frying pan 8 inches in diameter for preference.

4–6 servings:
6oz (180g, 1½cups) plain flour
2 eggs
pinch of salt
3tb (4tb) fine sugar
1pt (½l, 2½cups) milk
1tb wine, brandy or beer
butter for frying

The wine, brandy or beer is optional but it helps to make the pancakes crisp and naturally gives them a slight flavour of alcohol.

Sift the flour into a mixing bowl. Add the eggs, salt, sugar, milk and wine. Beat briskly to a smooth batter. The batter can be left for 30 minutes or used as soon as it is made.

Heat a thick frying pan until moderately hot. Test the pan: pour a few drops of cold water on it and when they dance in small beads on the surface the pan is ready. Very lightly rub the bottom of the pan with butter. Pour 1 to 2 tablespoons of the batter into the middle of the pan. Immediately tilt the pan back and forth so that the batter thinly covers the bottom. Fry over a medium heat until the pancake is lightly browned underneath. Loosen the edges with a spatula. Do not peek underneath to see whether the pancake is brown, this causes it to toughen. Turn the pancake and brown the other side. Stack on a warm plate. Keep warm in the oven until all are finished. Repeat with the remainder of the batter, buttering the pan lightly between each pancake.

Have your chosen filling ready in advance. When all the pancakes are finished, quickly spread each one with about 2 tablespoons of filling—do not over-fill or it will ooze out. Roll up and keep warm in the oven. Sprinkle lightly with fine sugar before serving. Or, after the pancakes have been filled they can be placed in a baking dish, brushed with beaten egg yolk and baked for a few minutes in a moderately hot oven (350°F: 180°C: Gas 4).

## PANCAKE FILLING (1) CURD CHEESE (*Török palacsinta töltelèk*)
### Hungary

4–6 servings:
4oz (125g,½cup) curd or cottage cheese
2–3tb cream
a few raisins, stoned
1tsp lemon rind, grated
sugar to taste
pinch of salt

Beat the curd cheese, moisten with cream (fresh or sour), add a few raisins, the lemon rind, sugar and salt. Instead of cream, the cheese may be moistened with brandy or rum.

## PANCAKE FILLING (2) WALNUT (*Diös töltelèk*)   Hungary

4–6 servings:
6oz (180g, 1½cups) shelled walnuts
sugar to taste

Finely chop or coarsely grate the walnuts and mix with sugar. Put a little of this mixture on to each pancake before folding it up.

Honey sometimes is used instead of sugar as it helps to bind the mixture.

## PANCAKE SOUFFLÉ (*Palacsinta felfujt*)   Hungary

4–6 servings:
butter, for greasing
12 pancakes (see page 165)
2oz (60g, 2tb) sugar
2tb raisins, stoned
2oz (60g, ½cup) almonds or walnuts, grated
3 egg whites
1oz (30g, 2tb) caster (extra fine) sugar
3tb (4tb) apricot jam

After frying the pancakes, roll them in the usual manner then cut into ½-inch wide strips. Arrange these in the baking dish. Sprinkle with the first quantity of sugar, add the raisins and nuts. Beat the egg whites until stiff, add the second quantity of sugar and continue beating until the egg white is of meringue consistency. Fold in the apricot jam. Spread this mixture over the top of the pancakes and bake in a moderate oven (350°F: 180°C: Gas 4) for about 10 minutes or until the meringue is firm and tinged with brown specks.

## PANCAKE 'PIE' (*Palacsintatorta*)    Hungary

4-6 servings:
10–12 pancakes (see page 165)
whole apricot or damson jam
bitter (baker's) chocolate, grated
finely ground nuts, hazel or walnuts
cream and raisins
4 egg whites
3oz (90g,⅓cup) sugar

Prepare all the pancakes. Place one on a warm plate and spread it with jam. Add a second pancake and spread it with grated chocolate (if liked, also with cream). Add a third pancake and spread this with nuts, a few stoned raisins and a little cream. Add the fourth pancake and continue in the same order until all the pancakes are used up. The top and final pancake must be left plain. Beat the egg whites until stiff, add the sugar and continue beating until the egg whites are very stiff. Spread this over the layered pancakes to completely cover them. Put into a hot oven (425°F: 220°C: Gas 7) and bake for a few minutes or until the meringue is tipped with brown. Serve cut into wedges like a cake.

## BAKED RICE PUDDING (*Reisauflauf*)    Austria

4–6 servings:
5oz (150g,¾cup) short grain rice
pinch of salt
½ vanilla bean
1pt (½l,2½cups) milk
2oz (60g,4tb) butter
3oz (90g,⅓cup) sugar
1tsp lemon rind, grated
2–3 egg yolks
2–3 egg whites
butter, for greasing
fine breadcrumbs, for sprinkling

Put the rice with the salt, vanilla bean and the milk in a pan and cook over a low heat until the rice is thick and soft. Take out the vanilla bean and leave the rice until cold. (Dry the vanilla bean, it can be used again and again.)

Beat the butter with the sugar until creamy, add the lemon rind and the egg yolks, beat well until the mixture is smooth. Beat the egg whites until stiff. Mix the creamed butter and egg into the rice then fold in the egg whites lightly.

Rub a large baking dish with butter, sprinkle lightly with breadcrumbs and add the rice. Bake in a slow oven (325°F: 160°C: Gas 3) for about 1 hour.

The pudding can be served plain or with a chocolate or raspberry jam sauce.

Or, instead of putting all the rice mixture into the prepared baking dish at once, spread only half the rice in it. Then add peeled, cored and thinly sliced apples, or apricot jam, or raisins, or peeled and sliced pears, or stoned cherries, or chopped nuts. Cover with the remaining rice and bake as above.


## FRUIT AND RICE MOULD (*Reis Trauttmansdorff*)   Austria

This dish was 'composed' for Ferdinand, Graf von Trauttmansdorff but by whom, why and when, is not known. The Graf was a member of an ancient Austrian family which came from the *Wienerwald*, the Vienna Woods.

4–6 servings:

4oz (125g,½cup) short grain rice

3oz (90g,⅓cup) sugar

pinch of salt

½ vanilla bean

1½pt (¾l,4cups) milk

1oz (30g,1envelope) gelatine

2tb maraschino

½pt (¼l,1¼cups) double or thick cream

4oz (125g,1cup) mixed candied fruit (approx)

Put the rice with the sugar, salt, vanilla bean and milk into a pan and cook over a low heat until the rice is tender. Take out the vanilla bean (this can be dried and used again). Let the rice cool.

Dissolve the gelatine in a little hot water and when completely dissolved let it cool, then add the maraschino and stir well. Whip the cream until stiff, add the dissolved gelatine, folding it in. Take half the candied fruit to use as a garnish, coarsely chop the remainder. Mix the rice into the cream, add the chopped candied fruit. Rinse a mould with cold water. Add the rice and cream mixture and put in a cold place to set. Turn out to serve, garnished with the remaining candied fruit and with a frothy wine sauce served separately (see page 129).

## EMPEROR'S PUDDING (*Kaiserpudding*)   Austria

6 servings:
6 bread rolls
½pt (¼l,1¼cups) milk
2½oz (75g,5tb) butter
5 eggs
3oz (90g,⅓cup) sugar
2½oz (75g,generous ⅓cup) almonds, ground
lemon rind, grated
2–3tsp vanilla sugar (see page 26)

Cut off the crusts from the bread rolls. Cut the soft portion into small cubes. (Instead of bread rolls, ⅓lb of white bread may be used.) Put into a mixing bowl. Warm the milk and pour it over the bread. Leave to soak while the other ingredients are being prepared.

Rub a large pudding basin with a little butter. Separate the eggs. Beat the remaining butter until soft, add 5 tablespoons of the sugar and beat until creamy. Add the egg yolks one at a time, beating well after each addition. Add the almonds, lemon rind and vanilla sugar. Squeeze the bread dry and mash free from lumps. Add to the creamed butter mixture and beat well. Beat the egg whites until stiff, add the remaining sugar and continue beating until the eggs have reached meringue consistency. Fold the egg whites into the pudding mixture and carefully mix until the batter is smooth. Pour into the buttered pudding basin. Cover with foil then with a white cloth, previously soaked in hot water and squeezed dry. Tie tightly with string round the rim of the basin. Put into a large pan with boiling water coming three-quarters of the way up the sides of the basin. Boil for 1½ to 1¾ hours, the water bubbling gently all the time. If the water appears to be boiling away too fast, add more boiling water to the pan.

To serve, remove the cloth and foil, turn the pudding out on to a hot round plate. Serve a frothy wine sauce (see page 129) separately.

## VIENNA NUT PUDDING (*Wiener Nusspudding*)   Austria

4–6 servings:
butter, for greasing
2oz (60g,½cup) hazelnuts or walnuts, finely ground
2½oz (75g,5tb) butter
2½oz (75g,5tb) fine sugar
3 egg yolks
3 egg whites
1¼oz (40g,5tb) self-raising or cake flour
3tb fine biscuit (cookie) crumbs

Rub a large pudding basin generously with softened butter and sprinkle lightly with half the ground nuts.

Beat the butter with 2 tablespoons of sugar until it is soft. Add the egg yolks and continue beating until the mixture is light and fluffy. Beat the egg whites until stiff then sprinkle in the rest of the sugar. Fold the beaten egg whites into the butter-cream alternately with the flour, nuts and biscuit (cookie) crumbs. Mix lightly but well then pour the mixture into the greased pudding basin. Cover with a cloth and tie with string securely round the rim. Put into a large pan with enough boiling water to reach three-quarters up the sides of the pudding basin. Cover and keep the water always just bubbling and check to see there is always enough water: if it boils away, add extra boiling water. Cook for 1¼ hours. Turn out to serve.

Serve with a frothy wine sauce (see page 129) or warmed apricot jam.

## PISCHINGER TORTE (*Pišingruv dort*)   Czechoslovakia

This is a good cake to serve at the end of a meal or at tea-time and is prepared with large, 8-inch-round wafers called *oblaten* (*oplatky*) which once were a speciality of Karlovy Vary, formerly Carlsbad, in Czechoslovakia. They are now prepared in other parts of the area as well as in the United States. They are available in Britain in specialist shops, in many of the better-class supermarkets as well as delicatessen stores. There are varieties of *oblaten*, some very small and crisp, others chocolate flavoured. For this recipe only the large *oblaten* are suitable.

4-6 servings:
10 oblaten wafers
5oz (150g,10tb) unsalted butter
8oz (250g,1cup) fine sugar
10oz (300g,10squares) bitter (baker's) chocolate, grated
vanilla flavouring to taste
¼lb (125g,scant cup) hazelnuts, finely grated
4 egg whites
6oz (180g,1½cups) icing (confectioner's) sugar

Place 1 *oblaten* on a round cake plate. Beat the butter until creamy and gradually beat in the sugar. Melt 6oz (6 squares; 180g) of chocolate in a bowl over boiling water. Beat it until smooth then add to the creamed butter and, when blended, add vanilla and nuts. Beat well. Beat the egg whites until stiff and fold into the chocolate mixture with a metal spoon.

Spread a thin layer of the chocolate mixture over the wafer in the plate, cover with a second wafer, spread this with a thin layer of the chocolate and continue in this fashion until all the wafers and the chocolate are finished. The top layer must be left plain.

Melt the remaining chocolate in a bowl over boiling water, add the icing (confectioner's) sugar, a little vanilla flavouring and about 2 table-spoons tepid water. Beat the mixture until smooth and spread over the top of the cake. Leave for 48 hours at room temperature.

## CHOCOLATE AND FRUIT 'SALAMI' (*Ovocný salám*)
Czechoslovakia

For 2–3 'salami':
4oz (125g,4squares) bitter (bakers') chocolate
4oz (125g,½cup) sugar
2oz (60g,⅓cup) almonds
2oz (60g,½cup) walnuts
½lb (250g) dates or figs
candied, or fresh, lemon peel to taste
1 egg, well beaten
icing or confectioner's sugar to taste

Heat the chocolate in the top of a double saucepan until it melts. Add the sugar and stir until it is dissolved. Finely chop the nuts, dates or figs and lemon peel and add to the chocolate. Very gently heat until the mixture is a thick paste that will form into a 'dough'. Add the egg and stir it well into the chocolate paste. Take the pan from the heat, turn the mixture out into a mixing bowl and beat until it cools. Shape into 2 to 3 'salami' sausages. Roll in icing sugar and then in foil or greaseproof paper. Leave in a cool place for about 24 hours.

To serve, cut aslant into thin slices. If necessary, the 'salami' can be stored for several weeks. But it is not advisable to keep it in the refrigerator although, out of necessity in a hot climate I have done this, taking it from the refrigerator a couple of hours at least before serving.

## STRÜDEL DOUGH (*Rètes*)  Hungary

Everyone knows that a *Strüdel* pastry is rich and composed of paper-thin dough with a filling which can be sweet or savoury, although for many people it means apple *Strüdel*. Generally it is considered an Austrian speciality but it is claimed by the Hungarians as one of their inventions, the pride of Hungarian cooks and housewives for centuries.

To be an expert in the art of making good *rètes* pastry is the ambition of every Hungarian cook. It must be as thin as gauze, without tears or slits, and the only secret of its preparation is to start learning how to make it when young, although I was also told not only youth is required but love and a prayer. The preparation of *rètes* requires at least four hands, six are even better.

Some essentials: the flour must be of the finest quality, neither too freshly milled nor damp. Well, we can insure against dampness, also ensure that it is/grade one flour and a strong flour with a high gluten content, but how freshly milled it is—that is something more difficult. Then a large kitchen table is required for the pastry has to be stretched and stretched by those extra willing hands which pull firmly but gently at the pastry in all directions.

For 12–14 slices:
1oz (30g,2tb) butter
½lb (250g,2cups) flour
pinch of salt
¼pt (1dl,⅔cup) warm water
1 small egg yolk
warm oil, for brushing
flour, for dusting

Melt the butter, let it cool but not harden. Sift the flour on to a pastry board in a mound. Make a hollow in the middle and add the salt and water. With a spatula blend the flour and water together to a firm dough, working from the outside edges inwards. Add the melted but cooled butter, the egg yolk and then begin to knead the pastry thoroughly with both fists and beat it again and again (my mentor said 100 to 150 times) until the dough is smooth and even slippery. Brush it with warm oil and leave it for 30 minutes on the board covered by a warm dish.

Put the kitchen table in the centre of the kitchen. Cover with a white cloth and flour it well. The cloth should be somewhat larger than an old-fashioned table napkin. Put the dough on the cloth and roll it out as evenly and as thinly as possible. There is a special long, thin rolling pin for this operation. Now at this point come those willing hands. Slip 2, 4, 6 hands under the dough, lift it and with the back of the hands, thumbs tucked in the fists, gently pull it in all directions until it comes just beyond the cloth and you can see through the dough. This must be done carefully otherwise it will tear. However, if it does tear, patch the holes carefully with the dough trimmed off to make the edges even. The edges are thicker than the rest of the dough, so when patching make sure these are rolled thinly.

When the dough is stretched to its fullest capacity it is ready for filling.

There are numerous fillings but here are the three most popular. The dough should be used within 5 minutes of stretching otherwise it will become dry. Therefore, the filling should be prepared while the dough is resting.

Apple *Strüdel* has become a favourite sweet dish not only in Central Europe but in the United States and, to a lesser degree, in Britain. So for those who blanch at all that love, care and youth used in the preparation of the dough, it is good to know that ready-made *Strüdel* dough can be bought in many food speciality stores.

Soft fried breadcrumbs are required for all fillings.

APPLE STRÜDEL (*Almàs rètes* or *Apfelstrüdel*)   Hungary

4–6 servings:
melted butter, for brushing
1½lb (¾kg) cooking apples
strüdel dough (see page 173)
2tb melted butter
2–3tb fried breadcrumbs
2oz (60g,¼cup) sugar
2oz (60g,⅓cup) stoned raisins
1oz (30g,2tb) blanched almonds, finely chopped
1tsp ground cinnamon

Peel and chop the apples and cook in as small a quantity of water as possible until very soft. Drain off surplus liquid.

Brush the dough with melted butter, spread evenly with breadcrumbs. Add the apples, sugar, raisins, almonds and cinnamon and spread evenly over the dough. Roll up by lifting the edge of the cloth on one side only and roll the dough as evenly and as tightly as possible, as for making a swiss roll. Gently lift on to a baking sheet. Brush the top with melted butter or, if preferred, with beaten egg yolk and bake in a moderate oven (350°F: 180°C: Gas 4) until the pastry is a golden brown, 35 to 45 minutes.

Serve sprinkled lightly with fine sugar and cut slantwise into 3-inch slices. Serve hot or cold—in Hungary *rètes* are served hot.

## MORELLO CHERRY STRÜDEL (*Meggyesrètes*)   Hungary

This is prepared in the same manner as apple *Strüdel* but Morello cherries, stoned and cooked, are used instead of apples.

Morellos are either black or dark red and very bitter. They are used only in cooking, for jams and preserves, and for distilling. Maraschino is made from Morellos.

## CURD CHEESE STRÜDEL (*Türos rètes*)   Hungary

4–6 servings:
1lb (½kg) curd or cottage cheese
2 egg yolks
2oz (60g,¼cup) sugar
2oz (60g,⅓cup) stoned raisins
1tsp lemon rind, grated
2 egg whites
strüdel dough (see page 173)
1oz (30g,2tb) melted butter
2–3tb fried soft breadcrumbs

Rub the curd cheese through a sieve into a mixing bowl. Beat the egg yolks with the sugar until smooth then beat in the curd cheese. Add the raisins and lemon rind. Beat the egg whites until stiff and fold into the curd cheese. Brush the dough with melted butter, sprinkle with bread-crumbs and evenly spread the curd cheese filling over the top. Continue as for apple *Strüdel*.

# SALADS and CHEESES

### SWEET PEPPER SALAD (*Paprikasalàta*)  Hungary

This salad can be prepared with fresh peppers when in season but also
with paprika pepper preserved in brine, although the brine must first be
well washed from them. Canned peppers can also be used.

4–6 servings:
1lb (½kg) sweet peppers
¼pt (1dl,⅔cup) mild vinegar
1tb sugar
salt to taste

If using brined or canned peppers, do not add salt to the dressing.

Wash or wipe the sweet peppers, cut into strips discarding the seeds and
cores. Dilute the vinegar with a little water, add the sugar and salt and
bring gently to the boil. While still hot, pour over the peppers. Cool
and chill before serving.

The hot dressing helps to soften the somewhat tough skins of the
peppers, also it brings out their flavour, which is greatly enhanced if they
are first cut into four, the seeds and cores discarded and the pieces of
pepper speared on to a fork and held over a high flame until the outer
skin is blistered. Take from the flame, cool and pull off the blistered skin.

## ASPARAGUS SALAD (*Spàrgasalàta*)   Hungary

4–6 servings:
1lb (½kg) asparagus
2–3tb wine vinegar
parsley, finely chopped, to taste
salt to taste
½tsp sugar
2tb olive oil

Canned asparagus is used in this recipe.

Drain the asparagus and cut into 1-inch pieces. Discard any tough ends (use them to flavour a soup or stock) and arrange the pieces in a shallow dish. Mix the vinegar with the parsley and add salt and sugar. Mix this into the asparagus with some care as the delicate tips break easily, then add the oil.

Serve ice-cold.

## ASPARAGUS SALAD WITH HAM (*Spargelsalat mit Warmen Schinken*) South Germany

4 servings:
2lb (1kg) asparagus
1tsp salt
1tsp sugar
salt, pepper to taste
3tb olive oil
1tb wine vinegar
cooked ham, 1–2 thick slices
1tb chives, finely chopped

For this recipe the Germans use the very thick white asparagus. Cut off the woody ends and peel as far as the purple portion of the stalks. Tie in a neat bundle and place upright in a tall, preferably narrow, pan of boiling water. Add the measured salt and sugar. Cover and cook for about 20 minutes or until the tops are tender. Test carefully with a fork to see.

With equal care take the asparagus from the pan for the tips break easily if roughly treated, drain and place on an oval flat dish. Let them become cold.

Make the dressing. Put a little salt and pepper into a small bowl, add the oil and stir until the salt and pepper are dissolved. Add the vinegar, again stir and then add 2 tablespoons of hot asparagus stock. Pour this hot dressing over the asparagus and leave until the asparagus is quite cold but baste frequently with the dressing.

In the meantime warm the ham, it should not be piping hot. Sprinkle the asparagus with the chives and serve the two together.

This dish, say the southern Germans, is a poem.

### BEETROOT SALAD (*Rote Rubensalat*)   South Germany

4–6 servings:
1lb (½kg) cooked beetroots (beets)
3tb vinegar
3tb oil
salt, pepper to taste
pinch of sugar
caraway seeds to garnish

Peel the beetroot and cut into neat cubes or thin slices. Place in a salad bowl. Mix the vinegar, oil, salt, pepper and sugar together, pour this over the beetroot and toss lightly. Leave for several hours, preferably in a refrigerator, or even better overnight.

Serve sprinkled with caraway seeds.

### RED CABBAGE SALAD (*Vöröskàposzta salàta*)   Hungary

4–6 servings:
1 small red cabbage
1tsp salt
¼pt (1dl,⅔cup) vinegar
¼pt (1dl,⅔cup) water
1tb white sugar
pepper to taste
caraway seeds to garnish

Pull off the bruised outer leaves of the cabbage, cut away the thick stalk and shred the rest finely. Put into a bowl, sprinkle with salt and leave for about 30 minutes. Combine the vinegar, water, sugar and pepper and bring to the boil in a small pan. Pour this over the cabbage. Cool, then place in the refrigerator. Before serving, sprinkle lightly with caraway seeds.

If preferred, use half crisp white cabbage and half red. The method is the same, only the name changes to *Szineskàposzta Salàta* or mixed salad.

### CUCUMBER SALAD (*Uborkasalàta*)   Hungary

4–6 servings:
1 large cucumber
2tsp salt
3tb oil
2tb vinegar
½tsp sugar
½tsp black pepper
½tsp paprika pepper

Thinly peel the cucumber and cut into thin slices. Put into a bowl and sprinkle with salt. Cover and leave for 1 hour.

Put the oil into a small mixing bowl, add the vinegar and sugar and mix well. When the cucumbers are ready, squeeze the slices gently, a few at a time, discarding all the bitter salt liquid. Put them into a salad bowl, add the dressing and mix well. Sprinkle with black pepper and toss, then sprinkle with paprika pepper as a garnish.

Serve well chilled.

## LEEK SALAD (*Porreesalat*)  South Germany

4–6 servings:
6–12 leeks (depending on size)
2tb vinegar
3–4tb olive oil
salt, pepper to taste
pinch of sugar

Thoroughly wash the leeks, remove the green part but do not discard for most of it can be cooked and made into a soup. Cut the leeks into strips and cook in salted boiling water for 10 to 15 minutes or until tender. Drain well. Mix the vinegar with the oil, add salt, pepper, a pinch of sugar and a little of the water in which the leeks were cooked, there should be just enough dressing to cover the leeks.

Serve chilled.

## LETTUCE SALAD (*Grüner Salat mit Speck*)  Austria

4–6 servings:
1–2 cos lettuces
2–3 slices very fat bacon
salt to taste
1tb vinegar

Wash the lettuce, pull all the leaves apart and carefully dry. Shake either in a lettuce basket or in a piece of soft absorbent cloth. Dice the bacon, put into a small pan and cook over a low heat until its fat runs and it is crisp and brown. Drop the lettuce leaves into a salad bowl, sprinkle lightly with salt, add the vinegar and lightly toss. Pour the bacon plus its fat over the top, toss again lightly and serve at once.

A similar salad is served in Hungary.

## MUSHROOM SALAD GARDENER'S STYLE
### (*Gombasalàta kertesznè mòrda*)   Hungary

4–6 servings:
1lb (½kg) firm fresh mushrooms
½pt (¼l, 1¼cups) olive oil
1 very small onion, peeled and finely chopped
1lb (½kg) firm ripe tomatoes
salt, pepper to taste
juice of 1 lemon

Wash the mushrooms and cut into thin slices. Heat the oil, add the onion and the mushrooms and cook gently until the mushrooms are just tender. While they are cooking, peel and finely chop the tomatoes, discarding their seeds. Combine the mushrooms with the tomatoes, add salt, pepper and the lemon juice and serve ice-cold.

It is essential to use olive oil in this recipe, any other kind of fat will congeal when cold.

## POTATO SALAD (*Bramborový salát*)   Czechoslovakia

4–6 servings:
2lb (1kg) potatoes
1–2 pickled gherkins (depending on size)
1 large white onion, peeled and finely chopped
1 small sweet pepper, flesh cut into thin strips
2 eggs, hard-boiled

For dressing:
4tb olive oil
pinch each of salt, sugar
1tb mild vinegar
1tb continental mustard

Cook the potatoes in their skins until tender but not mushy. Cool and peel then cut into cubes but do not let them get cold. Chop the gherkins.

Combine the potatoes, onion, gherkins and the sweet pepper (do not forget to discard the core and the seeds from this). Make the dressing. Pour the oil in a bowl, add the salt and sugar and mix thoroughly. Add the vinegar, stir well, add the mustard and when it is all mixed to a smooth dressing, pour it at once over the potatoes. Slice or chop the eggs and add to the salad at the moment of serving.

### FRUIT SALAD OR COMPOTE (*Gyümölcssaláta*)  Hungary

Although this is called a fruit salad in Hungary and in other parts of Central Europe, we are more likely to think of it as a fruit compôte or, more prosaically, stewed fruit. But such salads are served in Central Europe very often with roast meats, poultry and game.

Favourite fruits are apricots, peaches, cherries, greengages, pears and apples. They may be served separately or mixed, according to taste and season.

The fruit is prepared, peeled and cut as required and carefully poached in a little water lightly flavoured with sugar—it must not be too sweet. Other flavourings are added, such as lemon peel and juice, fruit kernels, almonds, etc. The fruit is served cold, usually chilled.

### LIPTAUER CHEESE (*Liptòi körözött*)  Hungary

*Liptòi* is a soft or curd cheese made from goat or sheeps' milk and owes its name to the Liptau range of mountains, now in Czechoslovakia, where it was made. It is a cheese with a somewhat acid flavour and is always served as *Liptòi Körözött* or garnished cheese.

4–6 servings:

½lb (250g, 1cup) curd or cottage cheese

¼lb (125g, ½cup) butter

½tsp paprika pepper

½tsp caraway seeds

½tsp dry mustard

4 capers, chopped

½tsp chives or onion, chopped

1–2tb ale or beer

Rub the cheese through a sieve. Cream the butter, mix it into the cheese and beat again until smooth. Add the remaining ingredients, the quantity of paprika pepper must not be more than enough to colour the cheese a faint pink, and the beer just enough to loosen it.

Serve on a dish piled in a mound, surrounded by radishes and eat with thin slices of brown bread.

One or two mashed anchovy fillets may be added to the basic mixture.


## SPRING CHEESE (*Frühlingskäse*)    Austria

This is a little like Liptauer cheese.

4–6 servings:
½lb (250g, 1cup) curd or cottage cheese
¼lb (125g, ½cup) butter
1tb cream
chives, finely chopped, to taste
salt to taste
paprika pepper to garnish

Rub the cheese through a sieve. Soften the butter. Combine and beat until smooth. Add the cream and chives. Salt may be added, also finely chopped parsley, and a few caraway seeds.

Spread this thickly on slices of coarse brown or white bread and sprinkle with paprika.

# BIBLIOGRAPHY

## AUSTRIA

Beer, Gretel. *Austrian Cooking* (London, 1954)
Philpot, Rosl. *Viennese Cookery* (London, 1965)
Piepenstock, Marianne. *Österreichishe Küche* (Munich, 1969)
Plakolb, Ludwig v. *Die Wiener Küche* (Munich, 1968)
Rösch, Rudolf. *So Kocht man in Wien* (Vienna, 1956)

## CZECHOSLOVAKIA

Brížová, Joza. *Cooking the Czech Way* (London, 1934)
Froidl, Ilse. *Böhmische Spezialitäten* (Munich, 1971)
Jandacek, M. L. *Czech National Cookbook* (Illinois, 1961)
Charlotte G. Masaryk Society. *Czechoslovak Pastries* (New York, 1952)
Mikulicek, Maria. *Czechs in the Kitchen* (London, 1945)

## HUNGARY

Culinary Arts Institute of Chicago. *The Hungarian Cookbook* (Chicago, 1955)
Deeley, Lilla. *Hungarian Cookery* (London, 1938)
Gundel, Kàroly. *Hungarian Cookery Book* (Budapest, 1956)
Horvàth, Maria. *Die Paprika – Küche* (Stuttgart, 1958)
Kovacs, Tibor. *Kleine Ungarische Küche* (Zurich, 1958)
Teklics, Anna. *Ungarische Küche* (Munich, 1968)
Venesz, Jòzsef. *Nationalgerichte aus Ungarn* (Budapest, 1959)

GERMANY

Adam, Hans Karl. *German Cookery* (London, 1970)
Howe, Robin. *German Cooking* (London, 1969)
Kirchdorfer, Trudl. *Bayerische Spezialitäten* (Munich, 1968)
Kirchdorfer, Trudl. *Münchner Schmankerl* (Munich, 1968)
Metzelthin, Pearl V. *World Wide Cook Book* (New York, 1944)
Stobart, Tom. *Herbs, Spices and Flavourings* (London, 1970)
Waldo, Myra. *Round-the-World Cookbook* (New York, 1954)
Wezäta Förlag of Göteborg. *European Cooking* (Göteborg, 1958)

# ACKNOWLEDGEMENTS

It is always a problem to say thank you to the many people who help in the writing of a cookery book. Some may only proffer a sentence, or a single recipe, or just an idea which leads to other channels of information. Others correct the spelling of foreign names, or give chunks of culinary lore, or lend books. To thank all these individually is not possible and, indeed, some of my exiled friends prefer to remain nameless for varying reasons. But to them all I say a sincere thank you.

However, I would like to record my thanks to Hans Karl Adam of Rothenburg, one of Germany's best-known cookery-book writers and television cook. And on the official side I wish to express my gratitude to the Fremdenverkehrsverband für Wien.

# INDEX